REVELATIONS
of the
FATHER

Dr. Hope Eady

xulon PRESS

Dedication

This book is dedicated to My God
Who has fathered me, loved me, carried me,
encouraged me, sustained me and
Delivered me
Your grace and favor upon my life
Keeps me humbled and awe filled
You truly are
The Lover of My Soul!

Table of Contents

Acknowledgments

I want to thank my family for your continued love and support especially my mother, Eva Scott and my two sisters – Wanda and Nita. You three have been my support system and my prayer partners. Your encouragement and belief that I could be used by God to bless others has meant more to me than I have the words or vocabulary to express. I am truly humbled that God would plant me in your midst!

Thank you to Tonya Jackson, the best friend anyone could ask for. You have walked with me through ups and downs and ends and outs. You have helped to dry my tears and been a source of laughter, love, and true friendship. I look forward to hearing your voice go around the globe singing His praises.

Thanks to Pastor Samuel Giles, Pastor Ayanna Giles, Arik Chappell, Jasmine Douglas, Tonthalell Walters, Marcus and Lisa Knight, and Timothy Jackson, the remaining members of the Hope International Ministries (HIM) team. Thank you for praying, pushing, and provoking me to destiny, but most of all thank you for believing in and investing in my dreams. You all are awesome and bring me great joy!

Thank you to Pastor Alex and Elder Casey Jackson for showing me a father's heart in the natural realm and loving me into a place of wholeness.

Thanks to Apostle Buddy for your love and support.

Thanks to Dr. Mary Crum, your mother's love, for just who I am, truly reflects the Father's heart for me. You have embraced me as your own and it strengthens me daily.

Forward by Dr. Mary Crum

As an apostolic-prophetic leader and founder of The Life Center Church and Ministries for thirty years, it has been my privilege to raise up great numbers of prophets and prophetic people both nationally and internationally. I have seen many aspects and facets of prophetic ministry from these prophets, and Dr. Hope Eady is a particular joy and is one who stands out among them.

A young woman of wisdom, integrity, keen insight, and confidence in God, she doesn't falter in what she sees and hears from Him. When she has a vision, she immediately seeks God for what the vision means and just as quickly receives His answer. She easily flows in a powerful prophetic word and frequently sees visions. Her style is straightforward, refreshing, insightful, and scripturally documented.

Dr. Hope serves in the Body of Christ as a Prophet-Teacher, and both of these office calls and the grace upon them are evident in this book. She wants you to have the stability and knowledge of the Logos Word, while receiving the prophetic revelation. As she flows as a Prophet-Teacher and Leader all her gifts converge to inspire, enlighten, and provoke people to a deeper relationship and experience with God.

Dr. Hope opens each chapter with scripture to set the stage for the condition, hurt, longing, or situation that she was going through or experiencing at the time. Her forthright and relatable testimonies are not only encouraging, but they are moving and perceptive. She shares her heart and struggles that each person who reads it will be able to grow and have a closer relationship with the Lord that makes them more effective Kingdom people. She then shares the God-given vision where the Lord met her at the place of her need or challenge. Next, she shares the revelation about the heart and character of God that was demonstrated during the vision. She then concludes each chapter with a teaching that releases the fuller meaning of the vision and how it applies to each of us in walking out healing, deliverance, and wholeness.

As you read this book, you will relate on a very personal level. Get ready for God to begin to reveal, heal, and empower you personally in areas of your own life with Revelations of the Father.

Revelations of the Father

*And he said, Hear now my words: If there be a prophet among you, I the LORD will make **myself known unto him in a vision**, and will speak unto him in a dream.*
—Numbers 12:6

Paul's heart cry was "…that I may know Him and the power of His resurrection, and the fellowship of His sufferings, being conformed to His death" (Philippians 3:10). I believe God answered Paul's fervent request and allowed him to come into a revelation few Christians have — the revelation of who God is! Unfortunately, many of us think we know God. He seems a distant being that we spend our Christian lives trying to understand and to comprehend His ways. Why does He allow evil? Why did He create the devil? Why hasn't He answered my prayers? But I believe God wants to reveal His heart and character to His people that we may know HIM! In the Old Testament, He loved us from above, and men could not fully comprehend the depth, height, and breadth of His love and heart toward them. In the New Testament, He demonstrated His love by dwelling among us and dying for our sins, and yet many still could not comprehend the extent of His love. Now He has sent His Spirit to dwell within us. It is by the Spirit of God that we come to truly understand who He is. The natural mind cannot fully understand Him, and He often has to take us out of our comfort zones to more fully reveal Himself to us.

Since receiving Christ as my Savior, I have been blessed to experience vivid God-ordained visions. I originally wondered why the Lord spoke to me in visions so frequently as opposed to other methods such as dreams or an inner knowing or conviction. The LORD began to unction me to write down the visions I was receiving from Him. I viewed them as being very personal as most did not reveal some great revelation about the Body of Christ or End-time events. In other words, I didn't perceive them as being a prophetic word or revelation. It was not until much later that I grew to understand that God was not just giving me messages in these visions, but that He was revealing His very heart and character. God was giving me visions because He was making Himself known to me. Each vision, I found, revealed a different aspect of His character and His ways. Without my realizing it, God was bestowing a great blessing upon me. He was revealing Himself. So many times, we seek to hear what He is saying or to learn what He is doing in our lives and even in the lives of others. But God was revealing something far more important. He was revealing and unveiling who He is and He was doing it in such a way that my human-limited understanding could conceive the awesomeness of WHO HE is and not just what He does.

God has declared to Moses that He would speak to him and other prophets through dreams. But He said He would reveal Himself through visions. In a vision, He revealed to Isaiah His Holiness. He revealed to Ezekiel His Glory and His Restoration Power in visions.

To Jeremiah, He revealed His Judgment, and to Daniel, He revealed His Power and His Imminent Return. I invite you to read the following accounts of the visions God has shown me. Each vision reveals a different aspect of the God we serve. Do these visions capture Him in His entirety? Certainly not! They merely scratch the surface of the author and finisher of our faith. But they do reveal His heart toward His servants and His love for His children. These visions show His love, His kindness, His faithfulness, His dedication, and even His determination for us to know Him. I count it a great privilege to have witnessed these visions and a tremendous honor and humbling experience to be allowed to share them with you. It is my prayer that you will come to know the Father in a deeper, more personal way as you read them. God is intimately acquainted with us, and these visions are an invitation for each of us to become more intimately acquainted with Him. Further, I encourage you to open your heart and to allow the Father to unveil Himself, His Precious Son, and His Mighty Holy Spirit to you in new ways as you read the following revelations of the Father.

Out on a Limb

In the day of my trouble I sought the LORD: my sore ran in the night, and ceased not: my soul refused to be comforted.

I remembered God, and was troubled: I complained, and my spirit was overwhelmed. Selah.

Thou holdest mine eyes waking: I am so troubled that I cannot speak.

I have considered the days of old, the years of ancient times.

I call to remembrance my song in the night: I commune with mine own heart: and my spirit made diligent search.

Will the LORD cast off for ever? And will he be favourable no more?

Is his mercy clean gone for ever? Doth his promise fail for evermore?

Hath God forgotten to be gracious? Hath he in anger shut up his tender mercies? Selah.

> *And I said, This is my infirmity: but I will remember the*
> *years of the right hand of the most High.*
> *I will remember the works of the LORD: surely I will*
> *remember thy wonders of old.* —Psalm 77:2-11

I recall going through a season of great discouragement. It came immediately after a season of great sacrifice-financially, emotionally, and physically. In my weariness, I glanced at my circumstances as they appeared in the natural. I had given up my secular job to go work at my church, and my financial situation, which had not been good to start with, suddenly grew bleak. I had given all I had financially, and I was exhausted from laboring at my church. When I looked at my circumstances, it seemed like I was suffering needlessly. I was proverbially "sick and tired", and I was angry about feeling that way. I felt as though it was taking everything within me just to hold on and struggle my way through each day. It was during this season that the Lord gave me a vision of being out on a limb.

In the vision, I was high up in a huge tree. It had a very wide trunk, and there were a lot of large branches on the tree all the way to the top. I was high up in the tree. I could look down and see a long way, but I wasn't at the top because I could look up and see there was still a long way to the top. There I was suspended somewhere midway in the tree, holding on to one of the large branches. In the vision, I could feel my arms getting tired. I felt like letting go. I wanted to let go, but something in me wouldn't give up. Yet, I didn't have the strength to climb back toward the center or trunk of the tree. As I hung there, I could suddenly see Jesus. He was sitting on one of the branches close to the trunk of the tree. He was clothed in white. He began to crawl out on the limb where I was. He came all the way out and hung on to the same limb I was hanging onto. He then got very close to me. Our faces were only inches apart, and He stared intensely into my eyes. He sternly said, "Don't you give up on Me!" I was shocked. He looked at me and repeated, "Don't you give up on Me!" The floodgates broke and tears streamed down my face. Jesus gently took me into His arms and carried me back near the trunk of the tree. He then helped me to continue my climb.

At the conclusion of this vision, my circumstances had not changed, but I had changed. In the few moments it took to give me this vision, the Lord had strengthened me spiritually, physically, and emotionally. He renewed my faith. How? By revealing that He would go out on a limb just to get me. Jesus met me in the midst of my need and then took me beyond it. He didn't say, "Come back in the tree and then I'll help you!" He didn't yell at me from afar or send a message through anyone. He joined me where I was and confronted the real issue—my *faith*, not my circumstances.

This is similar to what the LORD did with Shadrach, Meshach, and Abednego (See Daniel 3). The LORD did not spare them from the fiery furnace. He showed up in the midst of the flames with them. Many times, we are so focused on our deliverance that we miss what God is revealing to us about Himself during the midst of the struggles. If God had spared Shadrach, Meshach, and Abednego from the fiery furnace, we would have missed the opportunity to see the Pre-incarnate Christ revealed in the midst of the trial. God could have changed my circumstances and not allowed me to feel like I was out on a limb. But then I wouldn't have had the revelation that He loves me enough to climb out there to get me.

I have often reflected back upon this vision during times of need or crises. And I am reminded of the voice of the Lord commanding that I not give up on Him. That is His will for each of His children—that we never give up on Him. He commands that we never give up on His love, His faithfulness, or His power. We serve a God who is always there. He is always ready to go with us into whatever fiery furnace or lion's den or jail cell or hospital room or even out on a limb. He is forever by our side. He is ready to encourage, to strengthen, to comfort, to support, or even to carry. He goes wherever we are, and we must never give up on Him.

Many of us desire great things from God. We desire to do great exploits in His name. We desire to experience great wealth and prosperity. We desire great ministries and businesses. But we have been challenged and oppressed and discouraged for so long that those desires are faint dreams we pull out periodically and play with only to hide them again in the back of our closets when faced with the challenges and oppositions that have become a part of our everyday life. What we once cheerfully believed God for is now an impossible fairy tale that we want but don't believe we can ever have. God is saying to us, "Look again at what I promised. Look again at those gifts and desires that I have planted within you. Look again at those prophecies that have been given to you. Look again at those things I whispered to you in prayer. Look again at My promises in My Word. Look again, but this time look through the eyes of faith." How do we open up our eyes of faith? There are three things we need to focus on:

1. Rehearse the Word, not your Circumstances
2. Pray God's Word
3. Silence the Voice of Doubt (From Without and Within)

Key Points:

1. Rehearse the Word, not your Circumstances

Many times we rehearse our circumstances instead of rehearsing our promises. We talk about how bad things are instead of thanking God for how good things are. We take ownership and acceptance of sickness and disease or even poverty — "I have this or I have that…" or "My _____ is acting up" or "I don't have…." We don't realize that with our very words, we are re-affirming our situation instead of proclaiming our victory. I'm not saying to lie, but I am saying make sure your words are not helping the enemy fight you. Yes, you may have been diagnosed with some sickness or disease. Okay, but don't start claiming it as your personal pet or buddy. You may have a diagnosis, but you also have a promise — "…for I am the Lord that healeth thee" (Ex 15:26b).

How are we able to rehearse the Word — by reading and studying it

Rom 10:17 KJV

So then faith cometh by hearing, and hearing by the word of God.

As we rehearse the Word, we increase our faith. And it is our faith that God responds to.

2. Pray God's Word

Whatever you are believing God for, find a Scripture to support it and then pray that Scripture to God until you get a manifestation. In 1 Kings 19:41, when Elijah prophecies rain, he tells Ahab to go celebrate. But Elijah goes to pray. He goes back to the top of Mount

Carmel—back to the place where God had just demonstrated His power—Elijah casts himself upon the ground and cries out to God for the fulfillment of what God just promised. He prays God's word back to Him. How do I know that? Because he has his servant to serve as a lookout—looking for any sign of progress or manifestation of God's word. While his servant watched, he prayed. When the servant reported the first time that there was nothing there, instead of getting discouraged, he just continued to pray and kept telling his servant to look again. Many of us, as we face opposition to what God told us, instead of getting discouraged and throwing up our hands, we just need to keep praying until fulfillment or completion comes. Elijah's servant looked seven times. Biblically, the number seven represents completion. We have to learn to pray God's word to completion. Don't stop praying until you see the manifestation of the thing you are praying for.

3. Assassinate the Voice of Doubt (From Without and Within)

We need to fill our lives with faith and assassinate all doubt. There are people the enemy sends into our lives to pollute us with doubt. These people can always be counted upon to tell us what can't be done and why. They constantly remind us of our limitations and our liabilities. When we get excited about God, they tell us it doesn't take all that. When we get a new idea, they point out why it won't work. They tell us we are not smart enough, gifted enough, anointed enough, wealthy enough, pretty enough, handsome enough. In other words, the enemy speaks through them to try to convince us that we are not ENOUGH.

When the enemy can't find someone from without to pollute us with doubt, he will try to work from within. He will fill your own mind with your limitations. He pulls out his resume of all your past mistakes. He reminds you how you prayed before and nothing happened or gave before and didn't receive a harvest or tried before and seemingly only met with defeat. We cannot entertain these thoughts and be effective. We cannot live on a diet of doubt and expect God to move in the midst of it. We have to assassinate doubt. How do we kill him? We kill him with the Word. We kill him with Praise. We kill him with Fasting. But we **must** kill him. Refuse to speak negatively about yourself or anyone else. Don't raise a criticism or a concern unless you're also bringing a solution on how to overcome it.

Notice when Jesus healed the man in Mark 8, He took him outside the village. Jesus led him away from what was familiar and comfortable, away from naysayers and doubters. He took him outside even of himself, so he could receive something he had never received before.

> *"I can get more out of God by believing Him for one minute than by shouting at Him all night."* –Smith Wigglesworth

It is time to look again and believe again. It is time to believe God again. We need to go back and dig out what God said and allow Him to breathe upon it again and resurrect it. We need to allow God to resurrect our hopes and dreams that we let die in the midst of adversity and disappointment. Like the man Jesus healed, we need to "look hard." We need to fully, not partially, receive what Jesus is doing in our life. We need to believe again and watch God show Himself strong in our behalf!

In Your Embrace

In Your embrace
That's where I'll abide

In Your embrace
I can hide

In Your embrace
That's where I'll be

No fear
No hurt
No pain can follow me

Into Your embrace
Where there is peace

In Your embrace
I can be free

Free from failure, mistakes and pain
Free from fear, heartache and shame

In Your embrace
That's where I'll be

In Your embrace
I'm truly FREE!

All Together Lovely

His mouth is most sweet: yea, he is altogether lovely.
This is my beloved, and this is my friend, O daughters of
Jerusalem.   —Song of Solomon 5:16

I will praise thee; for I am fearfully and wonderfully made:
marvelous are thy works; and that my soul knoweth
right well.
My substance was not hid from thee, when I was made in
secret, and curiously wrought in the lowest parts of the earth.
Thine eyes did see my substance, yet being unperfect; and
in thy book all my members were written, which in contin-
uance were fashioned, when as yet there was none of them.
                                        —Psalm 139:14-16

For most of my upbringing and during my early adult years, I battled feelings of low self-esteem and insecurity. One partic-ular area that was especially difficult to overcome in this area was my feelings about my appearance. Being a dark-skinned African-American woman, fluctuating between dress sizes 10 and 14 and wearing a size 11 shoe, I didn't and don't exactly fit the "Barbie Doll" image of beauty. So I constantly felt I wasn't pretty enough. I thought my legs were too long and my torso too short. My feet and breasts were too big and backside was too flat. My skin was too dark; my eyes were too slanted; my cheekbones were too high, and I was too fat in general. I was constantly ready to point out all my faults. As a result, I hated mirrors and I hated shopping for clothes because stores usually had full-length mirrors. When I looked in the mirror, I saw my faults. I saw my weaknesses. I saw all the problem areas and why I wasn't pretty.

Not only did I see my physical flaws, but I saw my emotional and character flaws as well. I thought I was plain. I wasn't exciting, mysterious, and interesting enough. So I learned to hide to keep people from seeing my flaws and to keep me from having to constantly look at them. I learned to hide my emotions and to suppress my feelings and my thoughts. I built up layers of protective walls to keep people from getting close to me in fear that they would discover my imperfections and reject me because of them. I learned to fear the faces of men and to try to present myself in a way that would be pleasing unto them. All the time, I was suppressing the real Hope deeper and deeper into an abyss of fear, insecurity, and rejection.

Upon receiving salvation, of course, I immediately began to deal with God the same way I had dealt with people all my life. I continued to hide. Now not only was I afraid of what people would think, but I was now also constantly afraid of what the Lord had to say about me. He saw everything, so I was convinced that I was the lowliest of saints, that I had more sin and issues than anyone else and would never be good enough in God's eyes. So, I spent the next few years working even harder at pleasing people since it did not seem possible that I could ever win the war of trying to please God. I went to church day after day. I went to Bible Study on Tuesday nights. I even taught Sunday School and preached occasionally. And yet, I felt ugly, unattractive, and unworthy. I dodged mirrors, weight scales, and felt unworthy of being anyone's wife. I endured disappointing and painful dating relationships because I began the relationship feeling "lucky" that anyone would want to be with me.

I read books about overcoming low self-esteem. I stood in prayer lines and had ministers lay hands on me and pray for me to be delivered from low self-esteem and fear, and yet the battle raged within my mind. It had become almost a foundational belief for me that I wasn't enough. I wasn't good enough or smart enough or exciting enough. I was fully persuaded and thoroughly convinced that I was flawed, and therefore I was unlovable. I believed there was something about me that kept people and particularly men from loving me. Before salvation, I dated. There were even times when I received sexual propositions, but no one ever proposed. No one seemed to want me on a permanent basis—as a wife. For me, this only reaffirmed my belief that I was somehow unlovable and flawed. Each year, I sank deeper and deeper into a hole of self-rejection and people pleasing—not realizing that to reject myself was essentially to reject the God that created me. To embrace the enemy's lies that I was not enough was to bring an indictment against the One who created me—God. I did not begin the deliverance process until God gave me a divine revelation of the way He saw me.

In the vision, I could see myself walking through a meadow. The meadow had beautiful, lush, green grass and bright, colorful flowerbeds of every color imaginable. As I walked through the peaceful, still meadow, I came to a river that was completely clear, and it looked almost like glass. There were no ripples or waves — just perfectly still crystal clear water. As I stepped into the river, I immediately sank to the bottom, and I began to walk across the bottom of the river. There were smooth, even rocks lining the bottom of the river. When I got to the other side, I simply began to walk out of the river, but as I did, I noticed I was golden and glistening. Even my gown had changed from a stark white to a beautiful gold gown. My skin was gold. Everything about me was gold.

I then saw these elegant palatial-like white steps, which I climbed, and I entered into a building. I walked down a marble-floored corridor and approached a door, a large golden door. An angel clothed in white and holding a golden staff stood at the door and told me, "The King is waiting for you." He held open the door and I entered the room, which consisted of mirrors all around. I could not tell where the door was I had entered through because everywhere I looked there were mirrors. The only image reflected in the mirrors was me. I could see myself from every possible angle. I could see my front, my back, and both sides. Some mirrors were angled upward, and I could see what I looked like from the view of someone lying on the floor. Some mirrors were angled downward, so I could see what I looked like from the view of someone standing above me. I could see me from every angle, and yet there were no blemishes on me. Nothing was out of place. My gown of gold fit me perfectly. There were no wrinkles, no bulges, and no unsightly spots. Nothing about me was out of place or unbecoming. Then I heard the voice of the Lord say, "This is how you look to Me. I see you from every angle, and I know everything there is to know about you, and you are altogether lovely."

In this vision, God revealed His perfect love — His love that surpassed my fears. His love that serves as a banner and that covers all the multitude of my imperfections and flaws. It still amazes me that the most beautiful being of all, the Ancient of Days, could look at me and declare me altogether lovely. He showed me that His view and perspective is often very different from our own. When the lies of the enemy and the short-sightedness of men had devastated my self-image and esteem, God had to reveal His divine perspective.

It was interesting that He proclaimed me to be "altogether lovely." He did not call me pretty or beautiful or even cute. He called me "altogether lovely." I know the scriptural reference comes from the Song of Solomon 5:16, where the Shulamite declares:

> *His mouth is most sweet. Yes, he is altogether lovely.*
> *This is my beloved, and this is my friend, O daughters of*
> *Jerusalem!* (NKJV)

But I believe God was also addressing a deeper issue with me in His choice of the word "lovely." Lovely is defined as:

According to Webster's Dictionary,
1. Having such as appearance as excites, or is fitted to excite, love; beautiful; charming; very pleasing in form, looks, tone, or manner.
2. Lovable; amiable; having qualities of any kind which excite, or are fitted to excite, love or friendship.
3. Loving; tender.

4. Very pleasing;–applied loosely to almost anything which is not grand or merely pretty; as, a lovely view; a lovely valley; a lovely melody.

Adv. In a manner to please, or to excite love
According to Wordnet Dictionary,
1. lovely – appealing to the emotions as well as the eye
2. lovely – lovable especially in a childlike or naïve way
Synonyms: adorable, endearing

In calling me "altogether lovely", the Lord spoke not only to my physical appearance but to my entire being. He validated my worth, indicating that I have not only an appearance which excites, but that I am lovable. The Lord was letting me know that I was worthy of being loved — that I was designed to appeal to the emotions as well as the eye. He didn't say I was perfect. No human being is, but He let me know that because I am made in the image and likeness of Him that I am lovely. In other words, I too am deserving of love. I don't have to be movie star glamorous or plastic surgeon chiseled physical perfection. I need only reflect His beauty and love and character to the world, and in the process, I am transformed from sinful flesh into a woman who is

A- *Amiable*
L- *Loving*
T- *Tender*
O- *Original*
G- *Gracious*
E- *Endearing*
T- *Truthful*

H-   *Humble*

E-   *Elegant*

R-   *Rare*

L-   *Longsuffering*

O-   *Obedient*

V-   *Virtuous*

E-   *Exquisite*

L-   *Lovable*

Y-   *Yielded to God*

Key Points:

1. We Must Be Defined by the Word of God and Not the Opinions and Expectations of Men

When we don't know who we are in Christ, people and the enemy will try to determine who we are. For example, the children of Israel thought they were grasshoppers because they felt their enemy saw them as grasshoppers.

> **Numbers 13:31-33 MSG**
>
> 31 But the others said, "We can't attack those people; they're way stronger than we are." 32 They spread scary rumors among the People of Israel. They said, "We scouted out the land from one end to the other — it's a land that swallows people whole. Everybody we saw was huge. 33 Why, we even saw the Nephilim giants (the Anak giants come from the Nephilim). Alongside them we felt like grasshoppers. And they looked down on us as if we were grasshoppers.

So, instead of being defined by their God as "more than conquerors" or "giant-killers," they were defined by their enemy as grasshoppers. Too many times, we allow the lies of the enemy to define who we are and we take on identities that were never created for us like ugly, unattractive, defeated, un-loveable, or victim. We have to remember that we are created in the image and likeness of God.

> **Genesis 1:27–28 MSG**
>
> 27 God created human beings; he created them godlike, reflecting God's nature. He created them male and female.
>
> 28 God blessed them: "Prosper! Reproduce! Fill Earth! Take charge! Be responsible for fish in the sea and birds in the air, for every living thing that moves on the face of Earth."

2. Your Circumstances Do Not Determine Your Identity

We tend to want to define ourselves based on our physical appearance, income, family name, education, job titles, church titles, and positions or our health. However, our circumstances are a part of our testimony, not our identities. The Israelites saw themselves as grasshoppers in comparison to the size of their enemy. They defined themselves based on their circumstances. They focused on their limitations instead of God's ability.

3. Your Self-Image Determines Your Success

None of us can ever be successful being someone else because that is not who God created us to be. Our self-image determines how you think.

> Proverbs 23:7a KJV–For as he thinketh in his heart, so is he:
> The word translated as thinketh is sha`ar (shaw-ar'); means to split or open, i.e. (literally,) to act as gate-keeper; (figuratively) to estimate. What we think determines what we will become.

I cannot say that I have not had days when the enemy has tried to make me feel small, insignificant, and unattractive since this encounter with the Lord. But when the enemy does show up with his usual lies about who I am and tries to tell me I'm not enough, the Lord brings this vision to mind and I can hear the voice of my King saying all over again that I am "altogether lovely" in His eyes. When, as a single woman, my biological clock begins to alarm and family and friends ask the inevitable, "When are you going to get married? Are you at **least** dating someone?"; I am reminded that God wants me to know how valuable I am to Him, so that I won't settle for any mate that can't or won't agree with my God and my King in saying that I am "fearfully and wonderfully made" and I am "Altogether Lovely."

His Workmanship

I'm made in Your image and likeness

I look only like You could have imagined
My nose is uniquely shaped to inhale your sweet fragrance
My eyes are piercing and sharp to see in the Spirit
My lips are full and formed to smile and reflect your love
My voice is distinct and to be used for Your clarion call
My cheekbones are high and reflect Your precision
My skin is dark and comely and reflects Your rich workmanship
My neck is elongated to allow me to walk in Your grace
My shoulders are broad to carry Your Glory
My body is shapely and is used as an instrument of praise for only You
My arms are lengthy to do warfare in the Spirit and to better embrace Your
will for my life
My hands are strong and clap to your beat
My legs are long and equip me to walk in high places
My knees are prominent and are built for kneeling before You in prayer
and worship
My feet are big and beautiful because I publish Your Gospel and walk in peace

I embrace Your workmanship
Knowing that I was crafted in love and created for purpose

May I Have This Dance

The LORD thy God in the midst of thee is mighty; he will save, he will rejoice over thee with joy; he will rest in his love, he will joy over thee with singing. — Zephaniah 3:17

For as a young man marrieth a virgin, so shall thy sons marry thee: and as the bridegroom rejoiceth over the bride, so shall thy God rejoice over thee — Isaiah 62:5

One of the things I have struggled with in the past is truly understanding the breath and scope of the love of God toward me. For many years, my favorite song was a rendition of "Oh How I Love Jesus." It is usually thought of as a Sunday School song. But my heart would rejoice as I sang it. I believe I like it because it's a love song to Jesus. My favorite part was always the line, "Oh how **I** love Jesus!" It would remind me of how much I love the Lord and how important He is to me. One Sunday, I was in service and our minister of music was singing the slow worshipful arrangement of this song. As I lifted my head and whispered to God of my love for Him, He interrupted me. He pointed out that I was well aware of how I felt about Him, but I had not yet learned to receive His love. He said, "You like the part where it talks about how you feel about Me, but you haven't embraced that part where it says, 'Because He first loved me!" In other words, I was comfortable with my love for God, but I had not truly accepted His love for me. I knew my passion for Him and my desire to please Him, but I had not allowed Him to reveal His passionate, all consuming love for me. As I heard the words, the reality of them pierced my soul. I had not learned to receive God's love. I began to condemn myself yet again when the Lord showed me the following vision.

Suddenly, I saw a beautiful green meadow that I had seen before and a beautiful stream or creek that was as clear and still as glass. I again walked into the water and crossed the stream. On the other side were these beautiful glistening white steps. As I began to ascend the steps, I could see that my garment had been changed into a beautiful white robe. As I ascended each step, I could see blood running out from under the robe I had on. The blood did not stain the robe or the stairs. It just ran out from under the robe and back into the stream. As I looked up, I saw an angel standing at the top of the stairs; he informed that the Lord was waiting to see me. As I followed the angel, he led me again down a marble corridor and to a room with double doors. He then held out his hand, beckoning me to enter the room. When I entered the room, the Lord was there. He turned and looked at me. He said,

"You have no idea how much I love you. As passionate as
you are about me, I am that much more passionate about

36

you. My heart burns for you. I have not forgotten My promises to you. You are my Jedidiah. You are My Beloved. You are special and you are precious. You are loved passionately and deeply."

He then reached out and took me in His arms. And then we danced. He swirled me around the room in a beautiful waltz as He whispered words of love and comfort in my ear. I suddenly felt beautiful and cherished by the Lord Most High. The Lord told me I was special to Him—not because of any gifts or abilities I had, but because I am special to Him just as I am. He said,

"I made you. I am intimately acquainted with every aspect of you, and you are special and beloved to Me. I designed every part of you and you are pleasing in My eyesight."

I will forever cherish this revelation. We often picture God as a distant, disproving Father, who is waiting for us to make mistakes so He can rain down justice and vengeance upon our heads. But we serve a passionate God. He is passionate and fiery in His judgments, and He is also passionate and devoted in His love. God revealed that He is not only the "lover of my soul" but that I am "His Beloved." It is amazing what trials and issues can be overcome when we are equipped with the knowledge that we are loved deeply, passionately, and personally. The Lord was letting me know that I am not some member of a faceless crowd that He loves in general. I am His daughter that He knows intimately, and He is actively intervening in my life and my circumstances to perform His will. His focus is not just to accomplish some master plan, but in fact His mind, His will, and His emotions are consumed with thoughts of me and how to bless me and how to express His love for me.

John 3:16 NIV

"For God so loved the world that he gave his one and only Son, that whoever believes in him shall not perish but have eternal life.

Romans 5:8 NIV

But God demonstrates his own love for us in this: While we were still sinners, Christ died for us.

No matter how much I love Him or long for His presence, He always loves me and longs for me more. I recall a time when I was going through a lot of difficulties, and I hadn't realized it, but apparently I hadn't genuinely laughed in a while. Something funny happened and I burst into laughter. Immediately, the Holy Spirit said, "I missed that." I was surprised and said, "Lord, You missed what?" His answer shocked me. He said, "I missed the sound of your laughter." I learned something that day. God loves us so much that He rejoices at the sound of our laughter. He rejoices over us with singing. He is consumed with thoughts about us. He has even numbered our hairs.

I heard Joyce Meyer compare the apostles Peter and John. She noted how Peter emphasized his love for God, but that John emphasized Jesus' love for him. John is the apostle that kept referring to himself as the **"disciple whom Jesus loved"** or in John 20:2, the **"Beloved Disciple"**. This phrase is used five times in the Gospel of John, but in no other New Testament accounts of Jesus. John

21:24 claims that the Gospel of John is based on the written testimony of the **"Beloved Disciple"**. I believe that John had a revelation regarding the love of God towards us. He knew he loved Jesus, but he also understood that Jesus loved him and all that that means.

Key Points

1. God's Love is Unconditional

   Romans 8:35-39

   35 Who shall separate us from the love of Christ? Shall trouble or hardship or persecution or famine or nakedness or danger or sword? **36** As it is written: "For your sake we face death all day long; we are considered as sheep to be slaughtered."**37** No, in all these things we are more than conquerors through him who loved us.**38** For I am convinced that neither death nor life, neither angels nor demons, nei ther the present nor the future, nor any powers,**39** neither height nor depth, nor anything else in all creation, will be able to separate us from the love of God that is in Christ Jesus our Lord.

We often attach strings to our feelings for people. We love people who love us. We like people who like us. We love people who give us what we want or who behave the way we want them to behave. In other words, as long as you do what I want you to do, I love you. But according to **Luke 6:32 NIV**,

   "If you love those who love you, what credit is that to you? Even 'sinners' love those who love them.

God's love is not based on merit. Not even the most sanctified of persons deserves it. In **Luke 6:35 NIV**,

But love your enemies, do good to them, and lend to them without expecting to get anything back. Then your reward will be great, and you will be sons of the Most High, because he is kind to the ungrateful and wicked.

This is not a license to sin. Sin brings death and a bitter harvest just as righteousness has its rewards. But God's love is not based upon our behavior; it is based upon His nature. Does that mean that God loves you so much that He won't allow you to die in your sins and go to Hell? No, that means that He loves you enough to be born of a woman, live as a man, suffer and die one of the cruelest and most shameful methods of deaths, and be raised up again so that you wouldn't have to live or die in sin. His love provided our way of escape. All we have to do is receive it and live in it.

John 14:21 NIV
Whoever has my commands and obeys them, he is the one who loves me. He who loves me will be loved by my Father, and I too will love him and show myself to him."

When we truly love God, we want to obey Him. We want to follow Him, and His commandments are not grievous to us. When we truly receive His love and love Him in return—obeying Him brings us delight and He gives us the very desires of our heart (Psalm 37:4).

2. Acceptance of God's Love Empowers Us to Live Victorious Lives

In **Ephesians 3:14-21**, the Apostle Paul prays the following for the Ephesians:

> **16** I pray that out of his glorious riches he may
> strengthen you with power through his Spirit in
> your inner being,**17** so that Christ may dwell in your
> hearts through faith. And I pray that you, being
> rooted and established in love, **18** may have power,
> together with all the saints, to grasp how wide and
> long and high and deep is the love of Christ, **19** and
> to know this love that surpasses knowledge — that
> you may be filled to the measure of all the fullness of
> God.**20** Now to him who is able to do immeasurably
> more than all we ask or imagine, according to his
> power that is at work within us, **21** to him be glory
> in the church and in Christ Jesus throughout all gen-
> erations, for ever and ever! Amen.

Paul notes that it is as we are "rooted and established in love"
(verse 17) that we are empowered to understand the vastness of the
love of God (verse 18) and as a result are filled with the fullness of
God (verse 19). Understanding the depth, width, and height of God's
love for us empowers us to demonstrate His fullness in the earth.
According to 1 Corinthians 13, the gifts of the Spirit are designed to
work via love. The first fruit of the Spirit listed in Galatians 5:22 is
love. When we understand how great God's love is toward us, we
are able to operate without fear and its torment.

1John 4:18

[18] There is no fear in love. But perfect love drives out fear, because fear has to do with punishment. The one who fears is not made perfect in love.

When we truly receive the love of God, we are empowered to do His Will in the earth and to manifest His Power and His Presence for all to see.

3. We Cannot Fully Demonstrate the Love of God to Others Until We Have Truly Received It Ourselves

Romans 5:5 NIV

And hope does not disappoint us, because God has poured out his love into our hearts by the Holy Spirit, whom he has given us.

We cannot give away what we have not received. Until we receive the love God for us, it is difficult to demonstrate it to others. In the church my mother attends, they have a saying, "Now, that's love with work clothes on." In other words, someone has just done something to demonstrate love in action — love working. Love, like praise, is shown forth — it's demonstrated; it's seen.

John 13:1 NIV

[Jesus Washes His Disciples' Feet] It was just before the Passover Feast. Jesus knew that the time had come for him to leave this world and go to the Father. Having loved his own who were in the world, he now showed them the full extent of his love.

Jesus showed His disciples love by humbling Himself and performing the most menial of tasks by washing their feet. We are to demonstrate love to all we meet. We should be constantly thinking of ways to show love—a kind word, a pleasant smile, an encouragement card, a financial gift, treating someone to lunch or dinner, surprising a spouse or loved one with an unexpected gift just because it's Wednesday. There are countless things that we can do everyday to demonstrate love.

1 John 3:18 NIV
Dear children, let us not **love** with words or tongue
but with actions and in truth.

God loves us, so He gave His Son to come into the earth to redeem us. You are passionately and extravagantly loved. God loves you. Even if you don't get everything you want or can't give everything you would like to give—You are loved. The Creator of the Universe is in love with you and wants to empower you to do His Will. So, this day and everyday, rejoice in the God of your salvation. I know the enemy is fighting. He's fighting in our finances, our health, our families, on our jobs, and seemingly every place else. But you are not defeated. You are not alone—You are loved by the King of kings and Lord of lords. He's fighting in our finances, our health, our families, on our jobs, and seemingly every place else. But you are not defeated. You are not alone—You are loved by the King of kings and Lord of lords. He's willing to move heaven and earth to get to you. He promised in **Jeremiah 33:3 KJV**

3Call unto me, and I will answer thee, and shew thee great and mighty things, which thou knowest not.

Rejoice in His Love, rest in His love, regain your peace of mind in His love, and receive your answers in His love. There is supernatural provision in His love. There's wisdom in His love. There are divine strategies in His love. There's strength and hope in His love. Receive His love today.

1 John 3:1 NIV
How great is the love the Father has lavished on us, that we should be called children of God! And that is what we are! The reason the world does not know us is that it did not know him.

I encourage you to receive this revelation very personally. I believe God desires to empower you with the knowledge of how precious and beautiful you are to Him. He loves you deeply. He loves you passionately. His heart and His thoughts are directed toward you, and His thoughts toward you are GOOD. We do not serve a cold, distant God, but one who has a heart that beats for you. And He desires to dance with you today if you will open your heart and your arms and allow Him to lead you in His dance of love.

My Dance of Love

The music beats faster and faster
The thump of the bass drum reverberates in the house
The familiar rhythm tickles my toes
The chorus of Hallelujahs woos my feet to move
The celebration that creeps into my soul starts my legs to moving
The remembrance of Your faithfulness puts a swing in my arms
The promises of Your Word put a sway in my hips
And the joy of Your Salvation produces the dance…

The Dance of my Love.

Faithful & True

And I saw heaven opened, and behold a white horse; and he that sat upon him was called Faithful and True, and in righteousness he doth judge and make war.

His eyes were as a flame of fire, and on his head were many crowns; and he had a name written, that no man knew, but he himself.

And he was clothed with a vesture dipped in blood: and his name is called The Word of God.

And he hath on his vesture and on his thigh a name written, KING OF KINGS, AND LORD OF LORDS.

—Revelations 19:11-13, 16

I can recall, during a time of great stress and persecution, feeling all alone. As most of us have, I felt as though no one understood me or my plight. I had prayed, but I still did not *feel* the manifest presence of God and it almost felt as though He had finally left me, too. I had been misunderstood in the church I was attending. Seemingly those who should have known me best, in fact, apparently knew me least. I had come to the place of refusing to cry even unto God. I decided I had shed enough tears, and I was tired of being hurt and unappreciated. I withdrew into myself. Oh, I kept attending church and I even managed a smile every now and then; but on the inside, I deliberately let myself become cold, detached, and emotionally uninvolved. I rationalized that it would be better to be cold and withdrawn than to continually be wounded and discouraged. I decided to close my heart to those around me and to bide my time until I could escape to God only knows where. I frequently imagined getting into my car and riding off into the proverbial sunset. During this time, I went to the altar for prayer after an evening service. I do not remember what the altar call was for and I do not believe I had very high expectations for the prayer. I went up almost blindly, figuring it couldn't hurt. I am sure that laying hands on my forehead felt similar to laying hands on a brick. I was angry, cold, and hard. Eventually, the presence of God overshadowed me and I fell to the floor. When I did, the Father gave me the following revelation:

I could see a beautiful meadow with the greenest grass I have ever seen. There were beautiful flowers throughout the meadow and a peaceful stream wound tranquilly through it. There was also a lovely old tree that had beautiful white blossoms. Seated under the tree, lying on a blanket, was the Lord Jesus. He was dressed in white and leaned back against the trunk of the tree with His legs out in front of him. I could see myself dressed in a long, white robe. I was lying under the tree along with the Lord with my head resting in His lap. Suddenly, a gentle breeze blew and his garment billowed in the wind, and I could see indented upon His thigh the words— FAITHFUL AND TRUE. It was not branded or engraved upon Him. There was no scarring of His flesh. His flesh was indented to spell the words. It was not something that was put upon Him by someone. It was a part of who He is. It could not be separated from Him.

I do not recall Him speaking to me during this vision. The vision spoke for itself. Seeing Him being in a position of offering me comfort gave me a peace like I had never known. It suddenly did not matter that seemingly the world was against me. It did not matter that I was tired. It did not matter that I was hurt, frustrated, and angry. What did matter was that Jesus let me lay my head in His lap and rest. He comforted me with His presence. In the midst of the storm, He allowed me to steal away and rest with Him. He brought me to a place of peace where there were no deadlines or causes of stress. There were no motives to explain or actions to justify. There was no fear of what people were going to think about me or any pressure to perform according to anyone's standards. There was only peace and comfort. He did not tell me who was right or who was wrong. He did not even give me a strategy on how to solve the situation nor did He lecture me on the importance of forgiveness. He just let me rest— on Him and in Him.

Each of us, at some point in our walk with the Lord, will encounter challenges and difficulties that may seem overwhelming at the time. We may not feel prepared or we may wonder why this is happening to us or we may just be tired and frustrated with seemingly "going through" battle after battle after proverbial battle. And yet we know we can't quit. Giving in is not an option. It is easy to feel overwhelmed when you can't quit, but you're too tired to fight.

When we hit that place – that place of emptiness, frustration, and often pain; that place where our mouths can't even utter what our hearts feel; the place where we want to cry, but we're tired of crying; we want to run, but there seemingly is nowhere to run to; we want to scream, but feel that no one would hear us or if they did, they would not understand our heart cry – we have to decide to look to God.

Daniel 7:25 KJV

25 And he shall speak great words against the most High, and shall wear out the saints of the most High, and think to change times and laws: and they shall be given into his hand until a time and times and the dividing of time.

We are in an intense warfare, and if we are honest, many of us are weary of the fight. In Daniel 7:25, the Hebrew word which is translated as "wear out" is bela' (bel-aw') and literally means to afflict, but is used only in a mental sense. The enemy desires to wear us down. He desires to eat away at our faith and to try to destroy our relationship with Christ. He brings battle after battle, trying to bring us to a place where we quit and throw in the towel. Or he hopes to damage us so severely in the midst of the battles that we cannot be effective for the Kingdom of God. We must resist his efforts. This is not the time to quit or back up or go into hiding. Yes, the warfare has been intense. It seems like we are being fought on every hand – but God is greater than every situation that we face. We must resist weariness and choose to believe God again. We have to choose to believe Him despite what it looks like, despite what people say, even despite what our flesh is saying. We have to choose to believe God. We have to remember that God is who He says He is.

Key Points:

1. We Serve the Almighty God and He Cannot Lie.

God is who He says He is.

> **Deuteronomy 19:15 KJV**
>
> 15 One witness shall not rise up against a man for any iniquity, or for any sin, in any sin that he sinneth: at the mouth of two witnesses, or at the mouth of three witnesses, shall the matter be established.

In this passage, God has Moses establish a pattern for His people — that in the mouth of 2 or 3 witnesses, a matter would be established. This was designed to keep persons from bringing a false witness against another.

> **John 5:31-39 KJV**
>
> 31 If I bear witness of myself, my witness is not true.
>
> 32 There is another that beareth witness of me; and I know that the witness which he witnesseth of me is true.
>
> 33 Ye sent unto John, and he bare witness unto the truth.
>
> 34 But I receive not testimony from man: but these things I say, that ye might be saved.
>
> 35 He was a burning and a shining light: and ye were willing for a season to rejoice in his light.

36 But I have greater witness than that of John: for the works which the Father hath given me to finish, the same works that I do, bear witness of me, that the Father hath sent me.

37 And the Father himself, which hath sent me, hath borne witness of me. Ye have neither heard his voice at any time, nor seen his shape.

38 And ye have not his word abiding in you: for whom he hath sent, him ye believe not.

39 Search the scriptures; for in them ye think ye have eternal life: and they are they which testify of me.

1 John 5:6-10 KJV

6 This is he that came by water and blood, even Jesus Christ; not by water only, but by water and blood. And it is the Spirit that beareth witness, because the Spirit is truth.

7 For there are three that bear record in heaven, the Father, the Word, and the Holy Ghost: and these three are one.

8 And there are three that bear witness in earth, the spirit, and the water, and the blood: and these three agree in one.

9 If we receive the witness of men, the witness of God is greater: for this is the witness of God which he hath testified of his Son.

10 He that believeth on the Son of God hath the witness in himself: he that believeth not God hath made

him a liar; because he believeth not the record that God gave of his Son.

So in John 5 and in 1 John, we see God abiding by His own pattern of two or three witnesses establishing a matter. Jesus works, God the Father, and the Scriptures bear witness or testify of Him that He is who He says He is. In Heaven, the Father, Son, and Holy Ghost bear witness of each other. On earth, the spirit, the water, and the blood testify that God is who He says He is. 1 John 5:9 declares that the witness of God is greater than the witness of men. In other words, what God says overrides what men have said. According to Romans 3:3-4a,

> **Rom 3:3-4 KJV**
> 3 For what if some did not believe? shall their unbelief make the faith of God without effect?
> 4 God forbid: yea, let God be true, but every man a liar…

So for the former card players, what God says is trump. His Word trumps everything else on the table. God's Word is greater than the doctor's diagnosis, the loan officer's denial, the judge's sentence, the boss's decision, the foreclosure notice, the pain in your body, the ache in your heart, and even the disappointment in your mind. His Word is greater than what it looks like, more powerful than how it feels, and more true than what men would say. He reigns sovereign and He has the final say about you. He is who He says He is:

- In Genesis 1:1, He declares He is Elohim, the Creator and Sustainer of all that exists

- In Genesis 15:2, He declares He is Adonai, our Lord and Master
- In Genesis 14:18, He declares He is El Elyon, God Most High
- In Genesis 17:1-2, He declares He is El Shaddai, God Almighty
- In Genesis 2:4, He declares He is Yahweh or Jehovah, our Lord, our Covenant God
- In Genesis 22:14, He declares He is Jehovah Jireh, the Lord who Provides
- In Exodus 15:25-26, He declares He is Jehovah Rophe, the Lord our Healer
- In Exodus 17:15-16, He declares He is Jehovah Nissi, the Lord our Banner
- In Leviticus 20:8, He declares He is Jehovah Mekadesh, the Lord who Sanctifies you
- In Judges 6:24, He declares He is Jehovah Shalom, the Lord is Peace
- In Jeremiah 23:6, He declares He is Jehovah Tsidkenu, the Lord is our Righteousness
- In Psalm 23:1, He declares He is Jehovah Rohi, the Lord is my Shepherd
- In Ezekiel 48:35b, He declares He is Jehovah Shammah, the Lord is There or ever-present with us.

He is I AM that I AM. In other words, not only is God what you need Him to be when you need Him to be it, but moreover, He is Who He Says He Is. And there is none like Him.

The Father gave me a new understanding of what Jesus meant when He said,

> Come unto Me, all you who labor and are heavy laden, and I will give you rest. Take my yoke upon you and learn from Me, for I am gentle and lowly in

heart, and you will find rest for your souls. For My yoke is easy and My Burden is light.

—Matthew 11:28-30

I had become heavy with the hurt and offense and the circumstances of life. I was weary of the warfare, and the Lord allowed me to lay my head in His lap and rest. I had allowed myself to become depleted and empty, and He filled me up again. Not with my own strength, but with the strength He alone can provide. Often times we try to be so self-sufficient and self-sustaining that we forget that God did not promise you that your strength was enough. He declared that His Grace was sufficient. God does not expect us to stand alone up under the weight of the burdens of life. He expects us to cast those burdens upon Him and to allow Him to bear them as we walk with Him in obedience and faith and learn to rest in Him.

He also silently let me know that He had not left me nor forgotten His promises to me because He is faithful and true. It is not a character attribute that He possesses, but it is who He is. His faithfulness and the truth of His word are not based on outward circumstances, but they are based on who He is. As I lied on the floor during the middle of a service totally oblivious to all around me, the anger broke. The heaviness that had been upon my heart lifted, and my concerns about what had occurred floated away. In those brief moments, I transcended my circumstances. My focus was suddenly upon the One who was and is and is to come—the one who is always FAITHFUL and TRUE!

A Mystery to Me

This is a mystery to me...
The transformation of a butterfly hidden away in a cocoon
The diligence of a small ant
The melodious song of a bird

The beauty of praise with abandon
The fragrance of worship with passion
The power of prayer with faith

This is a mystery to me...
The sprinkling of the stars in the sky
The brilliant colors of the desert
The refreshing, ice cold waters of a mountain stream

The uniqueness of every human
The way of a mother with her child
The faithfulness of a loving God to His flawed creations.

The Master Surgeon

For the word of God is quick and powerful, and sharper than any twoedged sword, piercing even to the dividing asunder of soul and spirit, and of the joints and marrow, and is a discerner of the thoughts and intents of the heart. —Hebrews 4:12

I am crucified with Christ: nevertheless I live; yet not I, but Christ liveth in me: and the life which I now live in the flesh I live by the faith of the Son of God, who loved me, and gave himself for me. —Galatians 2:20

Knowing this, that our old man is crucified with him, that the body of sin might be destroyed, that henceforth we should not serve sin. —Romans 6:6

Jesus is the only one that can empower us to overcome our pasts. He comes in as a Master Surgeon and cuts away the things of this world that keep us from being transformed into His likeness. He is intimately acquainted with our thoughts, desires, and motives. Even when we deceive ourselves, we cannot deceive Him. He does not desire that we hide our hearts from Him, but rather He desires that we willing lay on His operating table and allow the scalpel of His Word to pierce our hearts, crucify our flesh, and cut away those things that are not like Him.

It was during a Sunday morning service as I went to the altar for prayer that the Lord allowed me to witness His power as the Master Surgeon to transform me. The master surgeon divided me and removed those things that were hindrances to His will being accomplished in my life. Jesus, the Word made flesh, pierced my heart and revealed His ability to deliver and to discern my heart.

As my pastor prayed a prayer of deliverance over me, he prayed that the assignment of all demonic forces that had been sent against me would be cancelled and every generational curse would be bound. As he laid his hands upon my head, I fell to the floor, praying in tongues. My eyes were closed but I could sense a very bright light shining over my face. I heard a comforting voice say, "I'm here." Suddenly I could see Jesus kneeling over me. He was made of light, but I could see the outline of His features. He was smiling down at me. I heard Him say,

"It's Me. Welcome Home. I'm doing spiritual surgery
on you today. I could have sent an angel to do it, but
I wanted to do this for you personally."

I saw Him open me up from the chest area all the way down. Then I saw a closet. The closet had shelves on all three sides. This closet was filled with dust and junk. I saw the Lord remove all the items from the closet and set them outside the door into a bag. Once all the items were removed, I saw Him wipe down the shelves and remove all dust and dirt from the closet. He placed everything in the bag and then handed the bag to an angel. That angel quickly passed the bag to another angel. This occurred several times faster and faster, and the bag was quickly spirited away. Then I saw Jesus kneeling over me again. He took my hand and my spirit got up, and I looked back and I could see the remains of me, my body, still lying on the floor. When I looked again, the remains were in a body bag and someone was zipping the bag closed. I saw as they zipped the bag up over the face. It was my face. The body was then lying in a drawer similar to what a morgue would store a body in. The angels closed the drawer with the body inside. I heard a voice say, "It's the old you." I was concerned about the body being in a drawer instead of being buried. I didn'tspeak, but I thought, "I wonder if she can come back." Suddenly the drawer became a cremation furnace, and I saw the body consumed by the flames. I heard, "The fire of the Holy Ghost is burning it up." I looked at the new me, and I was clothed in priestly garments of gold. I heard the Lord say,

> "When you get up, you'll feel lighter. You'll even look lighter. Your life will never be the same."

Then I saw the Lord and me dancing in a waltz-like fashion in celebration. I heard the voice of the Lord say,

> "ARISE, woman of God, arise! Arise with healing in your wings! Arise, prophet of God, arise! This is

your year, your time, and your season, arise! Destiny is at hand!"

I heard Bishop T.D. Jakes say in a sermon once that sin is not the problem within the Body of Christ. He said that sin is how we medicate our pain. His point was that people often seek comfort and escape in sinful acts, whether it be drugs, promiscuity, fornication, drinking, etc. Therefore, he was suggesting that if we begin to address the underlying root issues — the pain, anger, disappointment, low self-esteem, child abuse, rejection, and numerous others — there would be no need for the "medication" of sin. If we are honest, there are many who are wounded in the Body of Christ. This inner pain may be due to negative life experiences. For example, someone who was badly treated by one or both parents during childhood or someone may have been sexually abused or perhaps just generally ignored — not properly valued and loved. The negative experience opens the door for emotional pain which the victim carries with them long after the damage occurred. If someone suffered rejection in childhood, as an adult they may find it difficult to love others, or perhaps they may experience depression or a negative life attitude due to the damage.

Many of us have learned how to live with our damaged-selves. We've adapted to survive in this life. We've learned how to hide our issues and struggles often because we are ashamed of them.

Genesis 2: 25 KJV
25 And they were both naked, the man and his wife, and were not ashamed.

The Hebrew word for "ashamed" used in Genesis 2:25 is bûwsh {boosh}, which means ashamed, confounded, or confusion. Before sin, the word of God indicates they were naked. I do not believe that were covered by the glory of God or a cloud or anything else because the Bible says they were naked. We as Christians, many times, try to get around this. But the Bible says they were naked. I believe they were not only naked physically, but they were also naked spiritually and emotionally. There was no guile or deceit in them. They had nothing to hide. They were in proper union with their father and creator, and they had nothing to be ashamed of. They could stand naked before the Father and each other. They did not have hidden agendas and dirty secrets and things they were hiding in their hearts towards each other. So, they could stand naked and transparent before God and man and have no shame. We find that shame does not enter into the hearts and minds of men until sin and bondage enters the lives of men.

After sin, the man and woman become ashamed. They are instantly aware that they now have something to hide. When they cover themselves with fig leaves, they are actually covering their natural bodies, but they are trying to cover themselves spiritually and emotionally. They are trying to cover themselves not only from God, but from each other as well. They're ashamed. They're ashamed of their rebellion against God. They're ashamed of their pride. They have things to hide now from God and each other. And they are ashamed of their dirty little secrets. So, we find that shame entered the earth and the lives of men as a result of sin.

Key Points:
1. **We cannot hide from God. Covenant requires transparency.**

We serve an omniscient God. He knows everything. But we sometimes use that as an excuse to not discuss our issues with Him—we hide in the fact that He already knows.

2. When we attempt to hide our issues from God, He cannot address them.

God asked Adam where was he. Adam had to come out of hiding and acknowledge what he had done.

3. The shadows are where the enemy works. God operates in light.

The Body of Christ is at a very strategic time where we are going to have to come clean with God, operate in the light, and allow Him to address our issues or we are going to die in the shadows, oppressed by the enemy.

4. God desires to deliver us from the hurt and roll away the shame.

Joshua 5:1-9 opens with God having just dried up the Jordan before the children of Israel. The children of Israel have wandered in the wilderness for forty years. Moses is now dead, and God has risen up a new generation which is to be led by Joshua to possess the promised land. This generation is not the adults that God delivered with the ten plagues and brought across the Red Sea. These did not grow up slaves, but rather they are the children and descendants of slaves.

After crossing the Jordan, God instructs Joshua to circumcise the children of Israel. This generation had not been circumcised prior to this because they grew up in the wilderness. This is significant because circumcision is a sign of covenant that is born in one's flesh. This clearly identified them as belonging to Jehovah. They bore a mark in their flesh as a sign of the blood covenant relationship they had with God.

Upon completion of being circumcised, the Lord instructs Joshua that He has rolled away the reproach of Egypt from the children of Israel and that the place where they are encamped is to be called Gilgal. The name Gilgal is derived from the Hebrew word "galal" (gaw-lal) which means to roll, to commit, to remove, or roll away. Gilgal was the place where God rolled away the reproach of Egypt from the children of Israel. What was the reproach? The word reproach used here is "cherpah" (kher-paw) which means disgrace or shame. In other words, God declared that He was removing the disgrace of their past. He was taking away their shame. What shame? The shame of having been slaves; the shame of having been tainted with the idolatry of Egypt; the shame of being the descendants of those who rejected the promise of God and had to wander in the wilderness for forty years; the shame of having been talked about by other nations who said their God could not and would not deliver on His promise.

We cannot afford in this season to play games with God. It is time to be transparent and lay your heart open before Him that He can bring healing where it is needed.

Isaiah 42:9
Behold the former things are come to pass, and new things do I declare: before they spring forth I tell you of them.

God is doing a new thing in you. Your future with God is not determined by your past mistakes or disappointments or even your shame about your past. God comes to free you today from the pain of old decisions, from the shame of past mistakes. God knows every-thing there is to know about you and yet loves you anyway.

If you are wounded as you are reading this, God wants to heal your heart. It does not matter how long ago or how recent the hurt occurred. God desires to reach in and fix your heart. Pray this prayer with me:

Lord, Jesus

I lay my heart bare before You today. I give you permission to reach in and heal every wound, every bruise, every cut, and every scar. I ask you to pour in the oil and the wine and to make me whole this very hour. Father, help me to forgive those who hurt me and to release all bitterness and anger. Father, help me to receive your healing virtue right now. Make me whole and complete in you. Help me to be the man or woman of God that You have ordained me to be. In Jesus Name! Amen!

We each have to have this type of encounter with our Lord, where we allow ourselves to be laid open bare and allow ourselves to be changed in the process. In this vision, the Lord didn't judge me for what was in the closet of my heart. He simply did what He does best — He cleaned it out and let the fire of His Holy Spirit burn it up. I encourage each of you to allow Him to perform surgery on you today — Your life will never be the same as result.

Open Up

Stretch your arms wide that I might fill them with My Grace
Open up your heart that I might fill it with My Love
Gaze into the distance that I might fill your eyes with My Vision
Exercise your faith that I might fill your life with My Substance
Fling open the doors to your spirit that I might fill it with My Fruit
Open Up Again!

A Loving Touch

In the year King Uzziah died I saw also the LORD sitting upon a throne, high and lifted up, and his train filled the temple.

Above it stood the seraphims: each one had six wings; with twain he covered his face, and with twain he covered his feet, and with twain he did fly.

And one cried unto another, and said, Holy, holy, holy, is the LORD of hosts: the whole earth is full of His glory.

And the posts of the door moved at the voice of him that cried, and the house was filled with smoke.

Then said I, Woe is me! For I am undone; because I am a man of unclean lips, and I dwell in the midst of a people of unclean lips: for mine eyes have seen the King, the LORD of hosts.

Then flew one of the seraphims unto me, having a live coal in his hand, which he had taken with the tongs from off the altar:

And he laid it upon my mouth, and said, Lo, this hath touched thy lips; and thine iniquity is taken away, and thy sin is purged."　　　　　　　—Isaiah 6:1-7

I was in church in a worship service when the Lord gave me the following vision.

I was lying on the floor as was everyone in the church service. We were all lying prostrate on our backs under the anointing. As I looked up, I saw four angels fly into the sanctuary. They were each holding a corner of a gold sheet. The angels were completely golden. Their faces were gold, and they even wore gold gowns. Their heads were square or box-like in shape, and they had four faces — one in front, one in back, and one on each side. As they walked, they did not turn their heads, they just moved straight forward. They went around the room to each of the persons who were lying on the floor. As they went, they picked up little bundles off of each person and placed the bundles in the sheet which they had laid in the middle of the floor. After they finished collecting the bundles, they each again took a corner of the sheet, and they flew out of the building carrying all the bundles with them. I asked the Lord what were they doing, and I heard, "They are removing weights and hindrances from the people."

Then, I was suddenly in a clear plastic tube going higher and higher. I could see myself going higher. I went through the roof of the building, and still I ascended. I could see myself passing through the clouds. As I ascended higher and higher, I heard a voice say, "Up to the third heaven." I kept going higher until I reached a green meadow. All was very still and quiet. As I walked through the meadow, I saw a clear stream. It was perfectly still. The water was not moving or flowing, so it actually looked like glass. As I moved forward, I stepped into the stream. I immediately sank to the bottom, and I began to walk along the bottom of the stream to the other side. As I emerged from the stream, I noticed my garments had changed. I was now wearing a pure white robe. As I came up out of the stream, there were white stone stairs in front of me. As I walked up the stairs, I could see blood flowing out from under my garment and going back into the stream. My garment was not stained by the blood, but the blood continued to flow out from under my robe and back down the stairs into the clear stream.

When I reached the top of the stairs, there was an angel there waiting for me. He said, "The Lord is waiting for you." He then led me into a huge stone building. We walked down a corridor and came to two large gold doors. The doors opened, and I walked through into the Throne Room of God. I could see the Father sitting on His Throne. He was huge and filled the room. As I looked at Him, I could only see as high as His lap as he was seated there. There were seraphim flying around and singing praises. There were others who were kneeling and their foreheads were on the floor as they prostrated themselves in worship. There were others in the room who were singing and worshipping God. I found myself walking forward to stand before the Lord. As I did, I looked to my left, and standing at the Father's right side was the Lord Jesus. He was wearing a white robe and He stood smiling at me. The Father reached forward His right hand and caressed my cheek and said, "I see you; I know you, and I am well pleased." The Father then withdrew His hand, and I looked over at Jesus and He was still smiling at me. Then I walked out of the room and back down the corridor to the white stairs. I descended the stairs and walked back through the still river that looked like glass. I then saw myself descending in the glass tube until I was back in the Church Service.

> **Hebrews 10:22-23 NLT**
>
> 22 let us go right into the presence of God, with true hearts fully trusting him. For our evil consciences have been sprinkled with Christ's blood to make us clean, and our bodies have been washed with pure water. 23 Without wavering, let us hold tightly to the hope we say we have, for God can be trusted to keep his promise.

Key Points:

1. God Welcomes Us into His Presence

God expects and desires us to serve and pursue Him from one motive—LOVE, a sincere, pure and passionate love for Him. God does not want us coming to prayer for fear that if we don't, something bad will happen. He does not want us coming to service because our pastor or leader is expecting us. He wants us rushing excitedly into His house because we can't wait to see the one whom our souls love. He wants us in prayer because we can't bear to let a day go by without hearing our beloved's voice. He wants us worshipping and singing out of a joy that comes from knowing Him intimately. God does not want to bring hardships into your life to get you to spend time with Him. He wants to bless and, in the midst of the blessings, to receive your love.

Hebrews 10 speaks of our bodies being "washed with pure water." The Greek word translated as *wash* in this verse is:

- Wash- Louo (*loo'-o*) to bathe, wash

- of a dead person

- washing to cleanse blood out of wounds

This is the same word that used in **Revelation 1:5 (KJV)**

> **5**And from Jesus Christ, who is the faithful witness, and the first begotten of the dead, and the prince of the kings of the earth. Unto him that loved us, and washed us from our sins in his own blood,

2. God Sees Everything We Are Going Through

So often our flesh and the enemy try to convince us that we are alone — alone in our struggles, alone in our challenges, sometimes even alone in our victories. However, God is always there. Even when we can't trace Him or understand why He is allowing certain things in our lives, we have to yet trust His love and care for us. We have to take refuge in His Presence and seek Him even the more. We often seek Him for answers, "Why did my love one die?" or "Why is this so hard?" However, we have to learn to seek Him for His Presence. Although our natural inclination is, "Get me out of this, Jesus!", we have to develop and cultivate a spiritual inclination that says, "Let me see you, even in this Jesus!"

God wants to wash the blood out of your wounds. He wants to heal every wounded and broken place within us. He wants to remove sins and weights, but He also wants to heal our hearts and souls. God wants us to come into His presence and to grow and to look beyond our human limitations and to see and comprehend the awesomeness of an all-powerful, all-knowing, and ever-present God.

Whenever I read the book of Isaiah, I am always touched by the profound impact his encounter with the Lord had upon him. The Prophet Isaiah was never the same after he came face to face with the Lord. He was so changed by witnessing the angels cry, "Holy, holy, holy is the Lord of Hosts" that he later refers to God as the "Holy One of Israel." I know that God allowed me a tremendous honor to enter His Throne Room. It was not because I was worthy. Like Isaiah, seeing the Lord in His Glory made me that much more aware of my filth and unclean state. But this encounter also made me keenly aware of the love of God. He brought me into His presence to demonstrate His love and care for me. He could have rattled off a list of my faults and shortcomings, but instead He spoke of His care. He spoke of being intimately acquainted with me. He let me know that I was not a nameless face in some crowd, but that He was and is personally interested in me. He cares about what I care about. He comforted me and welcomed me into His Holy and awesome presence. And though I and no man or woman is worthy, He loves us enough to reach out His Holy hand and touch us and claim us as His own. Like Isaiah, my life will never be the same, and it is my prayer that after reading about this vision, your life will be forever changed as well.

We Crown You with Glory

We crown You with Glory
We enthrone You with Praise
We bow down before You
And lift up Your Name

We rejoice in Your Presence
We take comfort in Your Love
We demonstrate Your Power
And Your Glory from above

We crown You, Savior
We crown You, Lord
We crown You, Master
With one accord!

We speak well of You
And tell of Your Grace
We exalt You
Your Lordship we embrace!

Heart Fixer

For the hurt of the daughter of my people am I hurt; I am black; astonishment hath taken hold on me.

Is there no balm in Gilead; is there no physician there? why then is not the health of the daughter of my people recovered?   *— Jeremiah 8:21-22*

Be careful for nothing; but in every thing by prayer and supplication with thanksgiving let your requests be made known unto God.

And the peace of God, which passeth all understanding, shall keep your hearts and minds through Christ Jesus.
                                        — Philippians 4:6-7

I n Jeremiah 8, the Lord passionately expresses the depth of His love for Israel. He declares that He hurts when His people hurt.

So many Christians fail to understand the depth of God's love for us. We figure He is concerned about the Church or concerned about the pastor, but we often assume that God is not really interested in the daily affairs of our lives. However, according to Hebrews 4:15,

> *For we have not an high priests which cannot be touched with the feeling of our infirmities, but was in all points tempted like as we are, yet without sin.*

Jesus is concerned about every area of our lives — spiritual, physical, emotional, financial, and social. He is not just concerned about our spirit man. In other words, He does not desire us to be mighty spiritually, but sick in our bodies, emotionally wounded, financially poor, and lonely. He wants us to be whole in every area that we might serve Him effectively. When our hearts are wounded, it hinders our worship, our praise, and our ability to show love to others.

I recall coming to a place where I had been hurt in the church by Christians so many times that I barely wanted to go to the house of God. I could feel myself withdrawing from everyone. I was seemingly constantly being misunderstood or mistreated. My heart was wounded and my flesh wanted to just ride off into the sunset somewhere where no one would know me and no one could hurt me. I forced myself to come to church one night in spite of what I was feeling. I don't even remember what the sermon was about or the altar call, but somehow I found myself at the altar crying out to God. In the midst of my pain, I said, "Lord, They hurt me." His response was, "I know. Now let Me heal you." I then saw the Lord reach into my chest and pull out my heart. It was wounded. It had cut marks in it. Some cuts were precise like they were made with a surgeon's scalpel. Other cuts were jagged as though they were made with a butcher knife. There were dark bruises in some areas. My heart looked like it had been beaten with a stick or kicked around a room. I saw the Lord holding it in His hands. Then He began to smooth His right hand over my heart. As He rubbed His hand over my heart, where He rubbed was instantly healed. He ran His fingers over all the cuts and smoothed them away. He rubbed His hand over the bruises, and they disappeared. He continued rubbing His hand over my heart until every bruise, mark, and scar was completely gone. He then placed my new healed heart back within my body. And my flesh closed over where He had reached into me.

The word "heart" is used many times in Scripture, and we frequently use it in our society, but what does it really mean? The primary word used for heart in the Old Testament is "Leb" (*lave*). Leb and its synonym "Lebab" appear 860 times in the Old Testament. The books of the law, the prophets, and the Psalms often speak of the "heart."

"Heart" is used first of man in Gen 6:5: "And God saw that the wickedness of man was great in the earth, and that every imagination of the thoughts of his *heart* was only evil continually." In Gen 6:6, leb is used of God: "And it repented the Lord that he had made man on the earth, and it grieved him at his heart."

The word heart is used in reference to man or God in the following ways:

1. Physical Organ of the Body
   Examples:

- Ex 28:29–"And Aaron shall bear the names of the children of Israel in the breastplate of judgment upon his heart, when he goeth in unto the holy place...";
- 2 Sam 18:14–"...[Joab] took three darts in his hand, and thrust them through the heart of Absalom..."; and
- Ps 38:10–"My heart panteth..."

2. The Middle of a Thing

Examples:
- Ex 15:8–"...and the depths were congealed in the heart of the sea";
- Deuteronomy 4:11–"...and the mountain burned with fire in the midst [RSV, "to the heart"] of heaven..."; and
- Prov 23:34–"Yea, thou shalt be as he that lieth down in the midst of the sea..."

3. The Inner Man

Examples:
- Deuteronomy 30:14–"But the word is very nigh unto thee, in thy mouth, and in thy heart, that thou mayest do it" (cf. Joel 2:13); and
- 1 Sam 16:7–"...man looketh on the outward appearance, but the Lord looketh on the heart".

Lebab may be combined with "soul" for emphasis. For example, 2 Chron 15:12–"And they entered into a covenant to seek the Lord God of their fathers with all their heart and with all their soul." The word *Nepesh* (meaning soul, life, or self) is translated "heart" fifteen times in the KJV. Each time, it refers to the "inner man". An example is Prov 23:7–"For as he thinketh in his heart [nepesh], so is he."

4. Man or His Personality

    Examples:

- Gen 17:17–"Then Abraham fell upon his face and laughed, and said in his heart,...";

- Eccl 1:16–"...my heart had great experience..."; and

- Jer 3:15–"And I will give you pastors according to mine heart". {used in reference to God}

5. Origin of Desire or Will

    Examples:

- Ex 7:14–"Pharaoh's heart is hardened...";

- Ex 35:5–"...whosoever is of a willing heart, let him bring it...";

- Ps 86:12–"I will praise thee, O Lord my God, with all my heart..."; and

- Jer 32:41–"...and I will plant them in this land assuredly with my whole heart and with my whole soul" {used in reference to God}.

6. Source of Emotions

    Examples:

- Deuteronomy 6:5–"And thou shalt love the Lord thy God with all thine heart,...";

- Ex 4:14–"...and when he [Aaron] seeth thee, he will be glad in his heart";

- Judg 16:25–"And it came to pass, when their hearts were merry, ...";

- Isa 35:4–"Say to them that are of a fearful heart,…"; and

- 1 Sam 4:13–"And when he came, lo, Eli sat upon a seat by the wayside watching: for his heart trembled for the ark of God…"

7. Center of Knowledge and Wisdom

    Examples:

- Deuteronomy 8:5–"Thus you are to know in your heart...", NASB;
- Deuteronomy 29:4–"Yet the Lord hath not given you a heart to perceive [know]...";
- 1 Kings 3:9–"Give therefore thy servant an understanding heart to judge thy people, that I may discern between good and bad..."; and
- Job 22:22–"...lay up his [God's] words in thine heart."

8. Root of Conscience and Moral Character
      Examples:
- Gen 20:5–"...in the integrity of my heart and innocency of my hands I have done this";
- 2 Sam 24:10–"David's heart smote him..."; and
- Job27:6–"...my heart shall not reproach me as long as I live".

9. Seat of Rebellion and Pride
      Examples:
- Gen 8:21–"...for the imagination of man's heart is evil from his youth";
- Ezek 28:2–"Because thine heart is lifted up, and thou hast said, I am a God"; and
- Jer 17:1–"sin... is graven upon the table of their heart".

10. God Controls the Heart
      Examples:
- Ezek 36:26–"A new heart also will I give you,... and I will take away the stony heart out of your flesh, and I will give you a heart of flesh".
- Ps 51:10–"Create in me a clean heart, O God";
- Ps 86:11–"...unite my heart [give me an undivided heart] to fear thy name"; and

- 1 Chron 29:17–"I know also, my God, that thou triest the heart, and hast pleasure in uprightness". Ps 26:2–"...try my reins and my heart".

In the New Testament, the primary word used for heart is Kardia (car-dee-ah); where we derive the English word "cardiac" referring to the major physical organ. The word has come to represent man's entire mental and moral activity. In other words, the heart is used figuratively for the hidden depths of a person. Matt 15:19 and 20 describe human wickedness as in the 'heart' because sin has its origin in the center of man's heart and then 'defiles' or contaminates the entire being. Also, scripture describes the heart as the place of God's influence in Rom 2:15 and Acts 15:9. According to J. Laidlaw, in Hastings' Bible Dictionary, it "represents the true character but conceals it".

In the New Testament, the heart is described as:

1. Source of physical life–Acts 14:17; James 5:5;

2. Source of moral nature and spiritual life –(John 14:1; Rom 9:2; 2 Cor 2:4) including:
- Joy–John 16:22; Eph 5:19;
- Desires–Matt 5:28; 2 Peter 2:14;
- Affections–Luke 24:32; Acts 21:13;
- Perceptions–John 12:40; Eph 4:18;
- Thoughts–Matt 9:4; Heb 4:12;
- Understanding–Matt 13:15; Rom 1:21;
- Reasoning abilities–Mark 2:6; Luke 24:38;
- Imagination–Luke 1:51;
- Conscience–Acts 2:37; 1 John 3:20;

- Intentions–Heb 4:12, cf. 1 Peter 4:1;
- Purpose–Acts 11:23; 2 Cor 9:7;
- Will–Rom 6:17; Col 3:15; and
- Faith–Mark 11:23; Rom 10:10; Heb 3:12.

 In summary, our hearts are:
- inner man, mind, will, heart, understanding
- inner part, midst
- midst (of things)
- heart (of man)
- soul, heart (of man)
- mind, knowledge, thinking, reflection, memory
- inclination, resolution, determination (of will)
- conscience
- heart (of moral character)
- as seat of appetites
- as seat of emotions and passions
- as seat of courage

   This all reinforces that our hearts and their spiritual, emotional, and even physical state are very important to God and should be important to us as well. Often times as women, we are so busy taking care of others that we neglect to take care of ourselves and especially our own hearts. Somehow as women and especially as black women, we have learned how to make it. We have learned how to keep working, keep serving, keep moving, keep giving, keep smiling all while deeply wounded and hurting ourselves. Sometimes we are hurting physically, often hurting emotionally and spiritually. Many women in the church have become the walking wounded. Many of us are like the woman with the issue of blood. We try to act as though all is well and yet steadily lose life day by day — not admitting, not recognizing or acknowledging that our hearts are damaged or broken or bleeding.

Key Points:

Proverbs 4:23 KJV

Keep thy heart with all diligence; for out of it are the issues of life.

Proverbs 4:23 NLT

Above all else, guard your heart, for it affects everything you do.

Proverbs 4:23 Message Bible

Keep vigilant watch over your heart; that's where life starts.

Proverbs 4:23 Amplified

Above all else, guard your heart, for it is the wellspring of life.

Proverbs 4:23 New Century Version

Be careful what you think, because your thoughts run your life.

1. Whatever we allow to take root in our hearts will flow out into our lives.

Many of us are wondering why we have certain issues or certain struggles. It is because of what we have allowed to be planted in us. What does the enemy like to plant? The enemy likes to plant bitterness, strife, and contention. He likes to plant discouragement, doubt, and fear. He likes to plant envy, jealousy, and malice. He likes to plant wickedness, anger, and revenge. He likes to plant gossip, backbiting, and confusion.

> **Galatians 5:19-21**
>
> *19* When you follow the desires of your sinful nature, your lives will produce these evil results: sexual immorality, impure thoughts, eagerness for lustful pleasure, *20* idolatry, participation in demonic activities, hostility, quarreling, jealousy, outbursts of anger, selfish ambition, divisions, the feeling that everyone is wrong except those in your own little group, *21* envy, drunkenness, wild parties, and other kinds of sin. Let me tell you again, as I have before, that anyone living that sort of life will not inherit the Kingdom of God.

If he can keep us as women competing with each other and snarling with each other and tearing each other down, then we can never unite our voices in prayer and our hearts in worship and cast him out.

2. God has to uproot some things out of our hearts.

Matthew 13:24-30

24 Here is another story Jesus told: "The Kingdom of Heaven is like a farmer who planted good seed in his field. 25 But that night as everyone slept, his enemy came and planted weeds among the wheat. 26 When the crop began to grow and produce grain, the weeds also grew. 27 The farmer's servants came and told him, 'Sir, the field where you planted that good seed is full of weeds!' 28 "'An enemy has done it!' the farmer exclaimed."'Shall we pull out the weeds?' they asked. 29 "He replied, 'No, you'll hurt the wheat if you do. 30 Let both grow together until the harvest. Then I will tell the harvesters to sort out the weeds and burn them and to put the wheat in the barn.'"

For God to get His true harvest from your life, He has to at some point uproot the weeds or tares. The Lord has allowed you to go for a season with both wheat and weeds growing within you, but we are at the time of harvest. The weeds have to go. What God tolerated in the past cannot go with you in this new season. It is time for the weeds to be uprooted. He has to uproot those things that the enemy has planted, but you have to co-labor with Him. You have to be willing to lay your heart open before God and allow Him to show you what has been planted there so He can pluck out what needs to be removed and plant what needs to be planted. What does God want to plant in your heart?

Galatians 5: 22-23 NLT

22 But when the Holy Spirit controls our lives, he will produce this kind of fruit in us: love, joy, peace, patience, kindness, goodness, faithfulness, 23 gentleness, and self-control. Here there is no conflict with the law. 24 Those who belong to Christ Jesus have nailed the passions and desires of their sinful nature to his cross and crucified them there.

3. We have the responsibility of guarding our hearts.

We have to be diligent watchmen guarding the fields of our hearts and ensuring that the enemy does not plant ungodly seed. How do we guard our hearts?

a. We bring our thoughts into subjection to the Word of God

b. We chose to forgive daily. Not withholding forgiveness waiting for the person to repent or for us to be proven to be right. We put more emphasis on being right with God than with justifying ourselves.

c. We pray daily and keep our hearts humble before God.

d. We cultivate the fruit of the Spirit.

e. We pursue the heart of God like David did. David was a man who was after God's heart. In other words, he went after and pursued and chased the heart of God. He wooed God with worship. He sung God love songs. He wrote poetry to God. He loved on the Lord every chance he got. He wasn't casual about it or only sought God on Sundays. When he was in the palace, he worshipped. When he was hiding in caves, running for his life, he worshipped. When he sinned and messed up, he quickly repented and worshiped God for His Grace. We have to pursue God like David did.

"A woman's heart should be so hidden in God that a man has to seek Him just to find her." — *Maya Angelou*

God wants to be at the center of your heart. He wants to govern the seat of your mind, will, and emotions. He wants to determine what flows out into every area of your life and He wants what flows out to be of Him and not of the enemy. We have to allow God to purify our hearts and then we have to hide our hearts in Him.

When I walked away from that altar, I was no longer hurt. No one had apologized to me. No one had acknowledged that fact that they had hurt or wounded me, and yet I was whole and healthy because of what God did. In His concern and love for me, He moved to the core issue—I needed to be healed. To grow with the Lord—to do what He has called and commissioned me to do—I had to be healed.

So many times, we hinge our emotional healing on being vindicated or exonerated. We become so focused on: "Lord, show them I was right and they were wrong!" or "Lord, punish them for mistreating me!" that we miss the real core issue—you need to be healed! Regardless of who hurt you—saint or sinner; regardless of who was right, you or them, regardless of the motive, mistake or malice—you still need to be made WHOLE!

I had to realize there was too much at stake—too many souls are hanging in the balance for me to hang on to hurt. God had need of me, and for me to answer His call I needed to be healed. The Lord also revealed to me that He cares. He cares about my feelings. He cares about my disappointments. He cares about the state of my heart. And He is willing to heal. He desires to make us whole. We need only reach out to Him. He did not reach in and heal my heart until I went before Him and acknowledged that I was hurt. He is a heart fixer. No hurt is too great or too small for Him to address.

Enjoy the Journey

Enjoy the Journey
Enjoy the path

Enjoy each zenith
And each low
Enjoy it even when you don't know where to go

Enjoy the good times
And the bad
Enjoy it even when there seems no joy to be had

Enjoy the pit stops
And the marathons
Enjoy it even when you seemingly walk alone

Enjoy the fragrant flowers
And the bitter waters
Enjoy it even when you want to falter

Enjoy the friends you keep
And the ones that don't last
Enjoy it even when the expected betrayals come to pass

Enjoy wading in the quiet streams
And crossing the torrential rivers
Enjoy it even when everyone around you is taking and there
are no givers

Enjoy the quiet moments of reflection
And the noisy times of confusion
Enjoy it even when the notion of peace seems to be an illusion

Enjoy the gentle summer breezes
And the, hard freeze of winter
Enjoy it even when your faith in men seems ready to splinter

Enjoy the journey
Because I am with you!

The Deliverer

*For ye have not received the spirit of bondage again to fear;
but ye have received the Spirit of adoption, whereby we cry,
Abba, Father*   —Romans 8:15

*Stand fast therefore in the liberty wherewith Christ hath
made us free, and be not entangled again with the yoke of
bondage.*   —Galatians 5:1

*Forasmuch then as the children are partakers of flesh and
blood, he also himself likewise took part of the same; that
through death he might destroy him that. had the power
of death, that is, the devil;*

*And deliver them who through fear of death were all their
lifetime subject to bondage.*   —Hebrews 2:14-15

A ccording to Hebrews 2:14-15, Jesus through His death destroyed the power of death and the devil and delivered us from a lifetime of bondage. Many Christians have received salvation. That is, we know that we are not going to Hell. We know that we shall live eternally with Christ Jesus. But we have not understood or had the revelation that Jesus, through His death, burial, and resurrection also destroyed the power of the enemy over us and delivered us from a lifetime of bondage. There are so many Christians who should be free but who are actually enduring a lifetime of bondage. I know because I was one of them.

For years, I battled in my mind and in my thoughts. I would have cruel or ungodly thoughts, and I would condemn and beat myself up for weeks on end. If I made a mistake, I would berate myself. I would ask Jesus to forgive me, but for some reason, I could not seem to forgive myself. I worried constantly and could not enter the rest and peace of God. I could not truly see myself being used mightily of God or being strong spiritually. It was not that God could not do these things, but I had allowed the enemy to put me back into bondage in my mind. I could not see myself being whole, delivered, and set free in Jesus because the enemy was battling me in mind. As Joyce Meyer declared in her groundbreaking book, *The Battlefield of the Mind*, the mind is truly a battlefield for the saints. It is a place of intense warfare and conflict, and unfortunately it is often a place of defeat for the saints of God.

If we can allow Jesus to deliver our minds from bondage, it is extremely difficult for the enemy to keep us in bondage in any other area of our lives.

The Lord gave me a vision of my being delivered to remind me that He is still a deliverer. Just as he delivered the children of Israel from bondage in Egypt and then invested 40 years in the wilderness in delivering them from a "slave" mentality, the Lord wants to deliver us. He delivered us on Calvary's cross, and when we receive Him as Lord and Savior, He brings us out of Egypt. He then begins the process of leading us through our own personal wildernesses trying to deliver us from a "slave" or "bondage" mentality. How long we spend in our wilderness depends on how quickly we allow the Lord to deliver our minds. I stayed in my wilderness entirely too long, but the Lord was finally able to deliver me in my mind.

In a vision, I could see myself and I was seated in a wooden ladder back chair in a dark room. The room was completely dark except for one big spotlight shining down on me. It reminded me of an interrogation scene from some old *"film noire"* movie from the forties or fifties. The devil was standing behind the chair and he had me in a headlock — his arms were wrapped and encircling around my forehead. As I continued watching, a door suddenly opened in the darkness and Jesus entered the room. He was dressed completely in white. The enemy still had me in a headlock, but as I looked at Jesus, tears began to stream down my face. Suddenly, Jesus reached out His hand to me. I did not see Him touch me nor did I see myself rise from the chair, but instantly I was walking away with Jesus. As I looked back, the chair was empty except for a large chain that was lying in it. The enemy was gone, and I was free and walking on with Jesus. The darkness dissipated as Jesus and I walked away.

Key Points:
1. God is Our Deliverer and the Master of Our Breakthrough
2 Sam 5:17-25 NKJV

17 Now when the Philistines heard that they had anointed David king over Israel, all the Philistines went up to search for David. And David heard of it and went down to the stronghold. 18 The Philistines also went and deployed themselves in the Valley of Rephaim. 19 So David inquired of the Lord, saying, "Shall I go up against the Philistines? Will You deliver them into my hand?" And the Lord said to David, "Go up, for I will doubtless deliver the Philistines into your hand."

20 So David went to Baal Perazim, and David defeated them there; and he said, "The Lord has broken through my enemies before me, like a break-through of water." Therefore he called the name of that place Baal Perazim. 21 And they left their images there, and David and his men carried them away.

22 Then the Philistines went up once again and deployed themselves in the Valley of Rephaim. 23 Therefore David inquired of the Lord, and He said, "You shall not go up; circle around behind them, and come upon them in front of the mulberry trees. 24 And it shall be, when you hear the sound of marching in the tops of the mulberry trees, then you shall advance quickly. For then the Lord will go out before you to strike the camp of the Philistines." 25 And David did so, as the Lord commanded him; and he drove back the Philistines from Geba as far as Gezer.

The Hebrew word translated as breakthrough in this passage is **parats** (paw-rats'). It means to break out (in many applications, direct and indirect, literal and figurative). The KJV also translates this same word in other passages as — abroad, (make a) breach, break (away, down, -er, forth, in, up), burst out, come (spread) abroad, compel, disperse, grow, increase, open, press, scatter, urge.

BAAL-PERAZIM was a location near Jerusalem. David named the area Baal-perazim to commemorate the Lord's "breaking through" his enemies, since the phrase means the "lord of breaking through." A prophetic reference to a Mt. Perazim, where the Lord came "suddenly and in anger," may recall David's battle with the Philistines (Isaiah 28:21). David acknowledged that God, the Lord, had broken through or burst forth upon his enemies. God wants to breakthrough for us. He is the Lord of the Breakthrough and He desires to burst out, spread abroad, and scatter our enemies. God desires to increase us and open avenues and destroy barriers in our lives. In verse 21, the Philistines were so busy fleeing they left their idols behind, and David and his men burned them.

2. We Have to Stay in Constant Communication with the Master Strategist

Throughout the warfare, David consulted God not only as to what to do, but how to do it. Often we are defeated because we get directions from God but don't wait to receive strategy or battle plans. We know that God wants us to open a business, but we don't ask what kind of business or the timing of the opening or are we supposed to have business partners. I'm not talking about looking for excuses to not do it, but genuinely seeking the face of God for a strategy to successfully complete our assignment.

3. We have to Be Vigilant in Resisting the Enemy

Even after the breakthrough, the enemy came back again. Many times when God gives us breakthrough, we think that is the end. We want to believe that the devil will leave us alone and never come back, but that is not the case. He didn't even leave Jesus alone and never come back. After unsuccessfully tempting Jesus, Luke 4:13 says the enemy departed from Jesus for a season. When the enemy tries to arise a second time, we should not be discouraged by it, but see it as an opportunity to gain an even greater victory. When the Philistines came back, God allowed David to push them back even farther and gave him an even greater victory. We cannot afford to become complacent or lackadaisical about our relationship with the Lord or our stance of victory. Jesus has gotten us the victory, but we have to walk it out and refuse to be entangled again in bondage.

God is bringing you to your place of breakthrough. The time for it is now! We want breakthrough to come in the midst of peace, but breakthrough comes in the midst of warfare. Your current warfare has been designed by the enemy to wear you out, but it has been allowed by God to give you breakthrough. God wants to burst forth upon your spiritual enemies like the breaking forth of water through a dam—with great force and power. Allow God to show Himself strong on your behalf and give you victory like you have never experienced before—greater opposition brings greater victory.

God is the master or the Lord of the Breakthrough. God wants to break forth on the enemies of His people the way that water breaks forth through a dam with a crack. And just as the force of the water widens the crack, so there is a greater outpouring of the water. God wants a greater outpouring of His Spirit to be evident in our lives. God wants to demonstrate His power on behalf of His people, but we must seek Him for the strategy for our victory and we must be willing to go to war until we see it manifest.

This Prayer I Pray

Breakthrough beyond my mind
Breakthrough anything that confines

Anything that confines my dreams or confines who I can be
Breakthrough that I might be free!

Breakthrough beyond my circumstances
Breakthrough anything that would limit my path

Anything that limits my progress or where I can go
Breakthrough that I might grow!

Breakthrough beyond my past
Breakthrough anything that ties me down

Any old hurt or any new pain or any wound repeated again and again
Breakthrough that I might serve Thee!

An Invited Guest

Now David said, "Is there still anyone who is left of the house of Saul, that I may show him kindness for Jonathan's sake?"

And there was a servant of the house of Saul whose name was Ziba. So when they had called him to David, the king said to him, "Are you Ziba?" And he said, "At your service!"

Then the king said, "Is there not still someone of the house of Saul, to whom I may show the kindness of God?" And Ziba said to the king, "There is still a son of Jonathan who is lame in his feet."

So the king said to him, "Where is he?" And Ziba said to the king, "Indeed he is in the house of Machir the son of Ammiel, in Lo Debar."

Then King David sent and brought him out of the house of Machir the son of Ammiel, from Lo Debar.

Now when Mephibosheth the son of Jonathan, the son of Saul, had come to David, he fell on his face and prostrated himself. Then David said, "Mephibosheth?" And he answered, "Here is your servant!"

So David said to him, "Do not fear, for I will surely show you kindness for Jonathan your father's sake, and will restore to you all the land of Saul your grandfather; and you shall eat bread at my table continually."

Then he bowed himself, and said, "What is your servant, that you should look upon such a dead dog as I?"

And the king called to Ziba, Saul's servant, and said to him, "I have given to your master's son all that belonged to Saul and to all his house.

You therefore, and your sons and your servants, shall work the land for him, and you shall bring in the harvest, that your master's son may have food to eat. But Mephibosheth your master's son shall eat bread at my table always." Now Ziba had fifteen sons and twenty servants.

Then Ziba said to the king, "According to all that my lord the king has commanded his servant, so will your servant do." "As for Mephibosheth," said the king, "he shall eat at my table like one of the king's sons." –2 Samuel 9:1-11 NKJ

A few years ago, everyone was preaching sermons about Mephibosheth. There were even books written about him as the Lord was restoring the truth to the Body of Christ of His Restoration power. Many times we have head or intellectual knowledge of something, but we don't have a spiritual revelation of how God intends for it to impact our personal lives. Most Christians would say they believe God is a restorer, but if you asked how has God restored them or how does God plan to bring restoration to their lives, unfortunately most of us would struggle. I too have struggled with the concept of Restoration. Oh, I know that God has restored me by saving me, but what else does restoration mean. According to Vine's Expository Dictionary, there are several Hebrew and Greek words that mean "to restore."

The Hebrew word used for restore in 2 Samuel 9:7 is *shuwb* {shoob}. This word means:

A. to turn back, return
B. to return, come or go back
C. to return unto, go back, come back
D. of human relations
E. of spiritual relations
F. to cause to return, bring back
G. to bring back, allow to return, draw back, give back, restore relinquish, give in payment
H. to bring back, refresh, restore
I. to bring back, report to answer
J. to bring back, make requital, pay (as recompense)

The Greek word for RESTORATION is:

apokatastasis (NT: 605), from apo, "back, again," kathistemi, "to set in order," is used in Acts 3:21, RV, "restoration" (KJV, "restitution"). It is used of a "repair" of a public way, the "restoration" of estates to rightful owners, a "balancing" of accounts.

There are three (3) other Greek words that also mean to restore:

1. apodidomi (NT: 591), "to give back," is translated "I restore" in Luke 19:8.

2. apokathistemi or the alternative form apokathistano (NT:600) is used (a) of "restoration" to a former condition of health Matt 12:13; Mark 3:5; 8:25; Luke 6:10; (b) of the divine "restoration" of Israel and conditions affected by it, including the renewal of the covenant broken by them, Matt 17:11; Mark 9:12; Acts 1:6; (c) of "giving" or "bringing" a person back, Heb 13:19. It is used of financial restitution, of making good the breaking of a stone by a workman by his substituting another, of the reclamation of land, etc. (Moulton and Milligan).to reconstitute (in health, home or organization)

3. katartizo (NT:2675), "to mend, to furnish completely," is translated "restore" in Gal 6:1, metaphorically, of the "restoration," by those who are spiritual, of one overtaken in a trespass, such a one being as a dislocated member of the spiritual body. The tense is the continuous present, suggesting the necessity for patience and perseverance in the process.

Based on these definitions, restoration is designed to be a total process. It should include a giving or returning back what you formerly had physically or in health, in wealth, in answers, in land, or in possessions. But it also means to recompense or to be compensated for the fact that things were taken away in the first place. The

Lord drove home the totality of His Restoration process in the following vision.

I saw a beautiful green meadow that I have seen several times before and the beautiful stream or creek that was as clear and still as glass. I again walked into the water and crossed the stream. On the other side were these beautiful palatial steps. As I began to ascend the steps, I could see that my garment had been changed into a gleaming gold robe. As I ascended each step, I could again see blood running out from under the robe I had on. The blood did not stain the robe or the stairs. It just ran out from under the robe and back into the stream. As I looked up, I saw an angel standing at the top of the stairs; he informed that the Lord was waiting to see me. As I followed the angel, he led me down a corridor and to a room with two large golden doors.

The doors opened and I entered. Inside was a huge banquet table that was laden with a feast. There was any delicious food the heart or rather stomach could desire laid out. There were people seated at the table, but no one was eating. The Lord Jesus was seated at the head of the table at the far end of the room from where the doors were. As I entered, He arose and came to meet me. He took my hand and ushered me to a seat that was waiting just for me. He sat me down at His table and said, "You are My Invited Guest and you are welcome here." He then went back to His chair and the banquet began. They had been waiting on me to arrive. As I looked around the table, I saw the faces of the others, but I did not recognize anyone. All the other guests were smiling at me as we all shared a banquet as Invited Guests of the Lord, Most High.

The Lord did for me what David did for Mephibosheth. He brought me to his table as His honored guest. To sit at His table is not only what we need, but it is everything our hearts desire. At His table, we are accepted and welcomed. There were no second class citizens at his table. None of the guests were there because they were so gifted or important. They had no well-known names. They had no prestigious backgrounds. They had no important families or wealth or riches to earn them a place at the Lord's table. They were allowed to be there on one basis and one basis alone — Jesus had invited them. Jesus invites each of us to take our place at His table — or place as a favored son or daughter. He invites us to step into our place of restoration and wholeness. When Mephibosheth sat at David's table, his legs were hidden. In other words, his flaws and frailties could not be seen. His past became unimportant. It didn't matter that he used to live at Lo Debar, hiding out in someone's house. It didn't matter that he had been dropped by those who should have cared for him. It didn't matter that he had lost his inheritance. What mattered was he was the King's honored guest. And as the King's guest, he received all that the King had for him — TOTAL RESTORATION.

Psalm 85:1-9 NIV

1 You showed favor to your land, O Lord; you restored the fortunes of Jacob.

2 You forgave the iniquity of your people and covered all their sins. Selah

3 You set aside all your wrath and turned from your fierce anger.

4 Restore us again, O God our Savior, and put away your displeasure toward us.

5 Will you be angry with us forever? Will you pro-
long your anger through all generations?
6 Will you not revive us again, that your people may
rejoice in you?
7 Show us your unfailing love, O Lord, and grant us
your salvation.

8 I will listen to what God the Lord will say; he promises peace to his people, his saints — but let them not
return to folly.
9 Surely his salvation is near those who fear him, that
his glory may dwell in our land.

10 Love and faithfulness meet together; righteousness and peace kiss each other.
11 Faithfulness springs forth from the earth, and righteousness looks down from heaven.
12 The Lord will indeed give what is good, and our
land will yield its harvest.
13 Righteousness goes before him and prepares the
way for his steps.

Webster's Dictionary gives us the following definitions:

Restore- to renew; rebuild; (1) give back, return; (2) to put or
bring back into existence or use; (3) to bring back to or put back into
a former or original state; renew; (4) to put again in possession of
something.

Restoration- (1) an act of restoring or the condition of being
restored; as (a) a bringing back to a former position or condition;

reinstatement; (b) restitution; (c) a restoring to an unimpaired or improved condition; (d) the replacing of missing teeth or crowns; (2) something that is restored; especially a representation or reconstruction of the original form (as of a fossil or a building);

The word of God in John 10:10 declares that the thief, the enemy, comes but to kill, steal, and destroy. But that Jesus came that we might have life and life more abundantly. Many of us have been being robbed. We've been robbed of spiritual things—love, joy, peace. We've been robbed of natural things—health, finances, homes, cars, lands, businesses. Some of us have been robbed secretly, where the enemy has crept in and stolen from us and we did not even realize it at the time. Others of us have been robbed seemingly at gunpoint, where we have watched the enemy stealing from us but felt powerless to stop it. But God desires to restore us to Himself and to restore those things that we have allowed the enemy to steal. The day of restoration and recovery is at hand.

Key Points

1. God wants to restore you, not to who you were before, but to His original state, His original plan for you.

One of the meanings of restoration or resurrection is a moral recovery of spiritual truth. God wants you to discover the spiritual truth of who He designed you to be. You are fearfully and wonderfully made. You are created in His image and His likeness. You look the way He designed you to look. You don't have to compete with anyone else. You just have to be uniquely you!

Who you were before was flawed, but the original plan of God for you and your life is perfect and complete. So, God desires to restore you not to how you were a year ago or ten years ago. He wants to restore you back to the original plan or the original design.

2. Jesus came to restore.

Throughout Jesus' ministry, He brought restoration. He died that mankind could be restored back into right relationships with the Father. He restored health to the woman with the issue of blood and the man by the Pool of Bethesda. He restored life to Lazarus and to Jairus' daughter. He restored faith to Mary and Martha. He restored deliverance to Mary Magdalene and the Syro-phonecian woman's daughter. He restored grace to the woman caught in the act of adultery. Everywhere He went, He was about the Father's business of restoring back to mankind what God had originally ordained for their lives.

3. Restoration impacts the following areas:
    a. Restoration of Favor (Psalm 85:1)
    b. Restoration of fortunes (Psalm 85:1)
    c. Forgiveness for iniquities and sin (Psalm 85:2)
    d. Restoration of relationship with God (Psalm 85:3-5)
    e. Revival (Psalm 85:6)
    f. Restoration of Joy (Psalm 85:6)
    g. Restoration of Love (Psalm 85:7)
    h. Restoration of Salvation/Deliverance (Psalm 85:7)
    I. Restoration of Peace (Psalm 85:8)
    j. Restoration of God's Glory (Psalm 85:9)
    k. Restoration of Faithfulness (Psalm 85:10-11)
    l. Restoration of Righteousness (Psalm 85:10-11)
    m. Restoration of Blessings (Psalm 85:12)
    n. Restoration of Harvest (Psalm 85:12)

Jesus desires to restore you today. You've been waiting on it and praying for it, and the time is now at hand. I decree to you prophetically tonight that God is restoring in this hour. He is restoring opportunities. He is restoring hope, faith, and belief. He is restoring health and wealth. We need to believe God to move mightily in our lives in this season. The time of restoration is at hand.

Washed Away

I've washed away the stain of sin
I've wiped off the clinging dust of shame
I've rolled away the reproach of bondage
I've made you in My Image again!

I've smoothed away every hurt and cut
I've healed every wound and disease
I've uprooted every seed of fear and doubt
I've made you in My Image again!

The Master Designer

Esther 4:1-17 NIV

1 *When Mordecai learned of all that had been done, he tore his clothes, put on sackcloth and ashes, and went out into the city, wailing loudly and bitterly.* **2***But he went only as far as the king's gate, because no one clothed in sackcloth was allowed to enter it.* **3***In every province to which the edict and order of the king came, there was great mourning among the Jews, with fasting, weeping and wailing. Many lay in sackcloth and ashes.*

4*When Esther's maids and eunuchs came and told her about Mordecai, she was in great distress. She sent clothes for him to put on instead of his sackcloth, but he would not accept them.* **5***Then Esther summoned Hathach, one of the king's eunuchs assigned to attend her, and ordered him to find out what was troubling Mordecai and why.*

6So Hathach went out to Mordecai in the open square of the city in front of the king's gate. **7**Mordecai told him everything that had happened to him, including the exact amount of money Haman had promised to pay into the royal treasury for the destruction of the Jews. **8**He also gave him a copy of the text of the edict for their annihilation, which had been published in Susa, to show to Esther and explain it to her, and he told him to urge her to go into the king's presence to beg for mercy and plead with him for her people.

9Hathach went back and reported to Esther what Mordecai had said. **10**Then she instructed him to say to Mordecai, **11**"All the king's officials and the people of the royal provinces know that for any man or woman who approaches the king in the inner court without being summoned the king has but one law: that he be put to death. The only exception to this is for the king to extend the gold scepter to him and spare his life. But thirty days have passed since I was called to go to the king."

12When Esther's words were reported to Mordecai, **13**he sent back this answer: "Do not think that because you are in the king's house you alone of all the Jews will escape. **14**For if you remain silent at this time, relief and deliverance for the Jews will arise from another place, but you and your father's family will perish. And who knows but that you have come to royal position for such a time as this?"

15*Then Esther sent this reply to Mordecai:* 16*"Go, gather together all the Jews who are in Susa, and fast for me. Do not eat or drink for three days, night or day. I and my maids will fast as you do. When this is done, I will go to the king, even though it is against the law. And if I perish, I perish."*

17*So Mordecai went away and carried out all of Esther's instructions.*

Exodus 3:1-11 NIV

1*Now Moses was tending the flock of Jethro his father-in-law, the priest of Midian, and he led the flock to the far side of the desert and came to Horeb, the mountain of God.* 2*There the angel of the* Lord *appeared to him in flames of fire from within a bush. Moses saw that though the bush was on fire it did not burn up.* 3*So Moses thought, "I will go over and see this strange sight — why the bush does not burn up."*

4*When the* Lord *saw that he had gone over to look, God called to him from within the bush, "Moses! Moses!"*

And Moses said, "Here I am."

5*"Do not come any closer," God said. "Take off your sandals, for the place where you are standing is holy ground."* 6*Then he said, "I am the God of your father, the God of*

Abraham, the God of Isaac and the God of Jacob." At this, Moses hid his face, because he was afraid to look at God.

7The LORD said, "I have indeed seen the misery of my people in Egypt. I have heard them crying out because of their slave drivers, and I am concerned about their suffering. 8So I have come down to rescue them from the hand of the Egyptians and to bring them up out of that land into a good and spacious land, a land flowing with milk and honey – the home of the Canaanites, Hittites, Amorites, Perizzites, Hivites and Jebusites. 9And now the cry of the Israelites has reached me, and I have seen the way the Egyptians are oppressing them. 10So now, go. I am sending you to Pharaoh to bring my people the Israelites out of Egypt."

11But Moses said to God, "Who am I, that I should go to Pharaoh and bring the Israelites out of Egypt?"

I t is easy to get caught up in the day-to-day cares of life. There is seemingly always something to be done – something to capture or draw our attention. Between the demands of family, ministry, work, friends, and society, many times at the end of the day it seems like there is nothing left – not even for ourselves; and so many of us toil our way through our years. We're so busy that we fail to take the time to take stock of what we have actually accomplished. Others of us are constantly looking at our accomplishments. We're constantly assessing our financial status, our positions and titles at work, our level of influence and promotion at church, the community we live in, the size of our house—all in an attempt to gauge or measure our success. True, it's good to know where you are, but many of us are looking at the wrong gauges. We're evaluating ourselves based on the world's standards instead of looking at ourselves through the light of God's word. Don't misunderstand me—God does not have a problem with you being blessed. He wants you to prosper financially, socially, emotionally, physically, and in every other way possible. But you were put in the earth to be more than just blessed. You were put in the earth to be a blessing! You were meant to impact this world that we live in for Christ.

The Lord said to me once, "If I allowed you to, you would walk lightly through this life—not disturbing anyone, but I've called you to leave a big footprint upon this earth. I've called you to make a difference." And He has called each of us to make a difference. How do we make a difference? We complete our assignment.

Each of us was put into the earth with a purpose. God had something He needed done, and He specifically created you to do it. It's not optional. It's not a good idea. It's an assignment. It's an assignment that, at the end of this life on earth, you will have to give an account for—and somehow I don't believe Jesus is going to accept any of our excuses.

As I was in prayer one morning, the Lord showed me myself lying down on a piece of red velvety fabric. As I lay there, a light shined down and pierced the fabric and began to cut around me to make an outline or pattern of me in the fabric. When I stood, the Lord draped the fabric upon me and it became a garment that I was wearing. It was a long red velvet gown that fit me perfectly. As I stood before the Lord, the garment was changed and became a gleaming set of armor that shined brightly in every direction. I was covered in armor from my head to my feet and held a shining shield in one hand and a gleaming sword in the other. As I looked at myself through His eyes, I knew I had been clothed or prepared for battle and for purpose. My garments and armor had been designed to fit me and me alone.

Just as God was showing me that He has designed and fashioned me for my God-given assignments, He has fashioned each of us to be able to uniquely accomplish what He created us to do. None of us look exactly alike or think exactly the same or function like clones because we each have been uniquely and divinely fashioned by God, the Master Designer. None of us are after thoughts, but we each have been crafted and honed and fashioned to do His Will and not our own.

> *Ephesians 1:11*
> *In Him also we have obtained an inheritance, being pre-destined according to the purpose of Him who works all things according to the counsel of His will,*

> *2 Timothy 1:9*
> *who has saved us and called us with a holy calling, not according to our works, but according to His own purpose and grace which was given to us in Christ Jesus before time began,*

Each of us has been created and called by the Father. Many of us may know our call, but we may not know our specific assignment. You may know that you're called to be a pastor or a prophet or an intercessor or an apostle. That's good, but who are you called to pastor, what kind of a prophet are you, or what is your assignment in intercession, or where is your apostolic work to be done? In other words, what are you supposed to do with that call—that's the assignment. Esther was called to be queen, but her assignment was to deliver the Jews. Moses was called to be a prophet, but his assignment was to lead his people out of Egypt, prepare them to possess the Promised Land, and establish them in proper relationship with the Lord. He had to organize a bunch of slaves into a holy nation. What have you been called to and what is your assignment?

Key Points:

1. Refuse to accept Limitations (Fear, Doubt, Unbelief, Lack of Finances)

Our first step in completing our assignment is to refuse to accept limitations. What are limitations? Limitations are anything that the enemy sends to try to hinder you from completing your assignment For example, fear can be a limitation. What if I fail? What if I'm not good enough? What if my songs or my books or my art or my cooking aren't good enough? What if people don't like the way I preach? What if the person doesn't get healed? What if I don't have the money? While all those questions are running through your mind, also ask this one. What if it does? We have to refuse to live in a box constructed out of the devices of the enemy and the opinions of men. We have to refuse to be limited to old ways of thinking and old ways of doing things. When Mordecai sent Esther word of the situation and told her to intervene, she legitimately feared for her life. No one was supposed to go before the king if not summoned — so her intercession could have literally cost her life. But Mordecai had to remind her that her life wasn't the issue her. The issue was the will of God and that this was her assignment. She was the one that God had strategically placed to intervene on the behalf of His people. If she didn't obey due to fear, God would still deliver His people, but she would have missed her assignment.

When the enemy can't find someone from without to pollute us with doubt, he will try to work from within. He will fill your own mind with your limitations. He pulls out his resume of all your past mistakes. He points out to you how you prayed before and nothing happened or gave before and didn't receive a harvest or tried before and seemingly only met with defeat. We cannot entertain these thoughts and be effective. We cannot live on a diet of doubt and expect God to move in the midst of it. We have to assassinate doubt. How do we kill him? We kill him with the Word. We kill him with Praise. We kill him with Fasting. But we **must** kill him. Refuse to speak negatively about yourself or anyone else. Don't raise a criticism or a concern unless you're also bringing a solution on how to overcome it. We can't allow limitations, real or imagined, to keep us from fulfilling our assignment. You have come "to the Kingdom for such a time as this."

2. Refuse to Hide in Complacency

It is often easy to be comfortable in uncomfortable situations. Most people who are poor don't want to be poor. It does not feel good to constantly live in lack and not enough. But many people learn how to be poor and become comfortable in it, because at least it is familiar. We have to make sure we don't become comfortable in disobedience. Because if we are not preparing for our assignment or fulfilling our assignment (especially if we know what it is), then we are disobeying. We cannot afford to be complacent. We cannot afford to sit back and wait for someone else to do what God created us to do. Someone is saying, "But I don't know what to do?" Then ask Him to show you, but don't just sit there and die—wasting away in frustration.

3. Refuse to Make Excuses

We have to refuse to give excuses for not doing what God created us to do. When God called Moses, the first thing Moses said was, "Who am I..." Instead of focusing who God is, he immediately focused on who he wasn't. He gave excuses about what if they don't believe him and that he didn't speak well and finally he just asked God to please send someone else. The prophet that God spoke to face to face with, the prophet who wrote the first five books of the Bible, initially tried to get out of being a prophet at all. We can't afford to make excuses. We can't afford to miss our assignment. There are other people who are ordained to be impacted by what we do for Christ. We cannot afford to make excuses. Allow God to breathe His purpose and destiny into your life with a fresh kingdom perspective. See your life as He sees it.

4. Know and Understand that You Have Been and are Being Prepared

We have to realize that everything we have gone through up to this moment in time, God has used to prepare you. This is the process. God will use even our adversities, challenges, and failures to form and shape us into something valuable that He can use.

He has been working on you. That's why we can say that all things are working together for our good—because God uses it to prepare us. Even our mistakes He uses to discipline us and teach us if we allow it. God prepared Esther and Moses. Esther spent over a year being purified and prepared to meet the King. Moses spent forty years in Egypt learning to lead a nation and another 40 years learning to live in the wilderness and be a shepherd. He spent 80 years being prepared for a forty-year ministry of transforming slaves into more than conquerors. Your sacrifices have not been in vain. Your suffering has not been in vain. The attacks you have endured and the tragedies you have survived have not been in vain—God has been using it. Every challenge, every opposition, every battle, He has been using it to train you, to discipline you, to instruct you, to make you ready to do His will in the earth.

5. Obey the Call and Assignment of God

It is time to obey. It is time to seek the face of God—not just for goose bump feelings and experiences, but for the strength and the grace to fulfill destiny. It is time to look again at what God has placed in your hands and ask Him for the strategies on how to use it for His glory. It is time to walk into purpose and destiny. It takes this. This is what God had in mind when He crafted you. When He was molding and shaping you, it was for such a time as this.

This is your time of destiny and purpose. Do not become weary or disheartened. It is time to arise and expect God to move on your behalf. It is time to expect victory and joy. It is time to believe God and release your faith to look for, anticipate, and faithfully expect the fulfillment of His exceeding great and precious promises.

Do you go alone? No, He goes before you—leading and guiding you, pushing back the forces of the enemy for you, strengthening you, sustaining you, encouraging you. For you to experience the fullness of His grace, you have to walk in the fullness of His will. Allow God to use your unique talents and gifts to bring glory to HIS name.

Do what you were created to do!

My Love Song

My Dance is a dance of Praise
My Song is a song of Love
My Worship is full of Passion
My Joy is to do Your Will

My heart was created to love You
My voice was created to praise You
My laugh was created to make You smile

My gifts are for Your Glory
My mind to know Your Ways
My eyes to behold Your Beauty
My words to proclaim Your Might

My love to draw men to You
My worship to draw You to me
My triumphs to show forth Your Goodness
My testimony to declare Your Power

I was created to love You!
I was designed to do Your Will!
I was crafted for Your Purpose!
And I will, I will!

A Nurturing Father

And I will be a Father unto you, and ye shall be My sons and daughters, saith the Lord Almighty.
— II Corinthians 6:18

Doubtless thou art our father, though Abraham be ignorant of us, and Israel acknowledge us not: Thou, O LORD, art our father, our redeemer; Thy name is from everlasting.
— Isaiah 63:16

Repeatedly in Scripture, God is referred to as our Father. To a patriarchal society like the Israelites, this would have been a very familiar, positive, and relevant image. For our modern society, where fathers are frequently absent from the home or may not be representative of a Godly father, this image of God as Father may be an unfamiliar or conflicting image. I grew up without a father. He died when I was 17 months old, so I have no recollections of him at all. My maternal grandfather was a meek but reserved man who spent more time at church and at work than he did with his family. So he did not really fill in as a father figure in my life. I seldom saw my paternal grandfather, so he did not serve as a close fatherly image either. When my mother remarried, the relationship was turbulent at best and left me with a fatherly image of a bossy, selfish individual who was abusive physically, emotionally, and verbally.

Therefore, upon receiving salvation and being told that God was my Father, I was horrified. In my mind, fathers were either abusive or basically absent. I did not know what it was to be a little girl and sit on her Daddy's lap and feel secure and safe. I had no memories of being the apple of my father's eye. So, I had difficulty receiving God as a Father. I kept waiting for Him to judge me and find me lacking or I expected Him to ignore me and expect me to take care of myself. I did not know how to relate to my Spiritual Father because I had never learned how to relate to an earthly father. I simply did not understand father-daughter relationships. They were foreign to me. And as a result, my relationship with God was hindered. After many years of pretending I knew God as my Heavenly Father, the Lord finally put a stop to the pretense and forced me to address this issue in my life.

I was in prayer at the time. I would like to say that I was in a deep place in prayer, but in actuality I was praying the surface prayers we all have at some point prayed. In other words, I was speaking a lot of words, but it felt as though they were just reaching the ceiling and bouncing back down to me. At this point, God interrupted my prayer meeting with the following vision:

I was being carried in someone's arms like a small child. When I looked up, I saw it was the Lord who was carrying me in His arms and He was smiling down at me. Then He held me up in the air above His head and He began to swing me around in a circle—the way a father would with His small daughter. We both began laughing. God was smiling up at me and I was in His arms. He then lowered me and hugged me to His chest, and He continued walking on carrying me. Eventually, He lowered me and placed my feet on top of His feet and then He began to waltz with me—as though I was a little girl dancing with her Father while standing on His feet. When I looked up, the Lord was smiling down at me and laughing with joy. And joy and peace bubbled up within me, and I laughed again with the Lord. But it was a different laugh. It was the laugh of a child without a care or concern or worry in the world. It was a laugh of peace and safety.

When the vision ended, I was amazed. I was amazed that God had taken pleasure in me and allowed me to take pleasure in Him as my Father. When he held me in the air in His arms—for once it was not a struggle to trust Him or believe Him. I felt infinitely safe. Why? Because I finally trusted Him as my Father; I could feel safe. During the vision, it had not occurred to me that God might drop me or let me fall. I trusted Him. I expected Him to hold me up and to keep me safe. In the course of this vision, God took me beyond a painful childhood and beyond the disillusionment of adolescence and even beyond the jadedness of adulthood. In this vision, he restored what had been missing from my life—the joy of a father's love and approval. Sadly enough until that moment, I had not realized the impact this lack had had upon me. Growing up without a father had, in fact, scarred me, but when God allowed me to experience Him as my father, He healed that scar. My ability to believe God increased exponentially. My trust in His love and faithfulness grew. And I learned to find pleasure in resting in His love and strength. I learned to bask in His presence not just as a worshipper or servant, but as a daughter — a daughter who is favored, pampered, and loved just for who she is.

Key Points:

1. God's Very Nature is Love

"God is Love", but how do we define it? The Random House Dictionary defines love as: (1) a profoundly tender, passionate affection for another person; (2) a feeling of warm personal attachment or deep affection, as for a parent, child, or friend; (3)sexual passion or desire; (4) affectionate concern for the well-being of others; (5) strong predilection, enthusiasm, or liking for anything.

The American Heritage Dictionary defines love as "an intense affection for another person based on familial or personal ties". Often this "intense affection" stems from a sexual attraction for that other person. We love other people, or we say we love other people, when we are attracted to them and when they make us feel good. Notice that a key phrase in the dictionary definition of love is the phrase "based on". This phrase implies that we love conditionally; in other words, we love someone because they fulfill a condition that we require before we can love them. How many times have you heard or said, "I love you because you are cute;" or "I love you because you take good care of me;" or "I love you because you are fun to be with"?

We continue to love our children through good times and bad, and we don't stop loving them if they don't meet the expectations we may have for them. We make a choice to love our children even when we consider them unlovable; our love doesn't stop when we don't "feel" love for them. This is similar to God's love for us, but as we shall see, God's love transcends the human definition of love to a point that is hard for us to comprehend.

According to Romans 5:8, "*But God commendeth his love toward us, in that, while we were yet sinners, Christ died for us.*" In this verse and in John 3:16, we find no conditions placed on God's love for us. God doesn't say, "As soon as you clean up your act, I'll love you;" nor does He say, "I'll sacrifice my Son if you promise to love Me." In fact, in Romans 5:8, we find just the opposite. God wants us to know that His love is unconditional, so He sent His Son, Jesus Christ, to die for us while we were still unlovable sinners. We didn't have to get clean, and we didn't have to make any promises to God before we could experience His love. His love for us has always existed, and because of that, He did all the giving and sacrificing long before we were even aware that we needed His love.

2. True Love Only Comes Through a Relationship With Him

As such, true love—God's love—can be summed up in this passage of scripture: "*Beloved, let us love one another: for love is of God; and every one that loveth is born of God, and knoweth God. He that loveth not knoweth not God; for God is love. In this was manifested the love of God toward us, because that God sent his only begotten Son into the world, that we might live through him. Herein is love, not that we loved God, but that he loved us, and sent his Son to be the propitiation for our sins. Beloved, if God so loved us, we ought also to love one another.*" (1 John 4:7-11)

If you want to know this love – true love – get to know God. He is ready to pour out His love on you, and He wants to teach you how to love others as He loves you.

God's love has been made known to us and now He stands at the door and knocks. It's up to every individual to either pursue a personal relationship with God or else reject Him outright. The only barrier between us and God's love is our own free will and Jesus Christ is the door. "Jesus answered, 'I am the way and the truth and the life. No one comes to the Father except through me'" (John 14:6). Salvation is a free gift bought and paid for by the blood of Christ. There is no other way. "…Do not set aside the grace of God, for if righteousness could be gained through the law, Christ died for nothing!" (Galatians 2:21).

Later, I once asked the Lord why He allowed me to grow up without a natural father. His response was unexpected – *"Because it forced you to receive a father's love from Me and Me alone. Because you had no earthly representative of a father, you had to allow Me to father you and as a result you have a deeper relationship with Me."*

Amazing Love

I'm amazed that you love me
That YOU seek me out wherever I go
That YOU pick me up whenever I fall
That YOU heal me whenever I'm broken
That YOU restore me whenever I've fallen short
That YOU encourage me whenever I want to quit
That YOU love me endlessly, passionately, sacrificially and unconditionally
Even in the midst of my imperfections

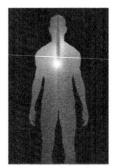

United as One

And all who have been united with Christ in baptism have been made like Him. —Galatians 3:27 NLT

But we all, with open face beholding as in a glass the glory of the Lord, are changed into the same image from glory to glory, even as by the Spirit of the Lord. —2 Cor. 3:18

God is changing and transitioning His People. His will is to change or transform us to look and to be more and more like Him. The Father re-affirmed this revelation in a vision He gave me.

I again saw the beautiful green meadow that I have seen several times before and the beautiful stream or creek that was as clear and still as glass. I again walked into the water and crossed the stream. On the other side were the beautiful white steps. As I began to ascend the steps, I could see that my garment had been changed into a glistening white garment. As I ascended each step, I could again see blood running out from under the robe I had on. The blood did not stain the robe or the stairs. It just ran out from under the robe and back into the stream. As I looked up, I saw an angel standing at the top of the stairs; he ushered me into the Lord's throne room. I again saw the Lord sitting upon His huge throne that filled the room, but I did not see anyone else. Jesus was standing at the right side of the throne and walked forward to meet me. He took me by the hand and led me to the left side of the throne where there was a door. The door was made into the very throne or seat where God the Father was sitting. When I entered this room, there was a huge blue flame or light in the center of the room that came up from the floor and arose high into the air like a huge column of blue fire. I stood there looking for the top of the flame and it seemed to never stop. Jesus again reached for my hand and led me toward the column of fire. He held my hand as he encouraged me to step into the midst of the blue flame. I stood in the midst of the flame, but it did not burn. As I stood there, I saw less and less of me. I began to become one with the flame. It was consuming me, but I was not being lost, I was just becoming a part of the flame and light until all I saw was the blue flame.

I know that God was showing me that He desires to transform me and each of us into His image and likeness. God desires to change or transition us into His vessels in the earth—that when people look upon us, they see Him. It is time to transition or change. Transition is defined as movement, passage, or change from one position, state, stage, subject, concept, etc., to another; change. We often pray for transition or change. We ask God to change our circumstances or situations. We cry out for new jobs, new homes, etc. Singles pray to be married. The poor pray to be rich. The rich pray to be richer. The unhappy pray for happiness. The discouraged ask for encouragement. We often ask God for change, but do we move and prepare to receive those things for which we are asking?

James 2:17

Even so faith, if it hath not works, is dead, being alone.

If we are asking God for blessings, for supernatural intervention, then should we not move in faith in expectation of His response? We must prepare ourselves to shift—naturally, spiritually, financially, and even emotionally. I am not talking about being so consumed with living for tomorrow that you forget to enjoy the today He blessed you with. But I am talking about preparing to go to the next level even while you are enjoying the benefits of where you are right now.

Key Points:

1. Preparing for Where We Are Going

We can enjoy preparing for our next state even as we are enjoying our present one. Even as we are believing God for a mate or for prosperity or for deliverance, true faith moves us to the action of preparing for those things.

Exodus 12:11 NIV

This is how you are to eat it: with your cloak tucked into your belt, your sandals on your feet and your staff in your hand. Eat it in haste; it is the Lord's Passover.

As God takes us places that we've never been and gives us experiences that we've never had, we must prepare ourselves for the new and not be caught up in business as usual. We don't want to miss our season of visitation because we have become comfortable with the old season. We must first allow the Word of God (the logos, rhema and dabar) to transform our minds to expect and prepare for a new move of God.

> **Romans 12:2**
>
> And be not conformed to this world: but be ye trans-
> formed by the renewing of your mind, that ye may
> prove what is that good, and acceptable, and perfect,
> will of God.
>
> We must plan and prepare for these spiritual seasons
> with the same vigor and enthusiasm that we invest
> in our physical seasons.

2. Knowing the Times and the Seasons

We need to sense what God is doing in our lives. Sense that you are operating in a new day and a new season—not just because somebody said it and not just because the date on the calendar changed, but because you are tuned into God for yourself. Just as we know and recognize when the seasons change in the natural:

- Spring Equinox – near March 21
- Summer Solstice – near June 21
- Fall (Autumn) Equinox – near September 21
- Winter Solstice – near December 21

We must recognize the changing of spiritual seasons.

3. You must Operate Differently in a New Season

You cannot operate in the Promised Land the way you operated in the Wilderness. If your season has changed and your territory has changed, then to be successful your tactics must change. It is often easy to be comfortable in uncomfortable situations. Most people who are poor don't want to be poor. It does not feel good to constantly live in lack and not enough. But many people learn how to be poor and become comfortable in it, because at least it is familiar. We have to make sure we don't become comfortable in disobedience. Because if we are not preparing for our assignment or fulfilling our assignment (especially if we know what it is), then we are disobeying. We cannot afford to be complacent. We cannot afford to sit back and wait for someone else to do what God created us to do. Someone is saying, "But I don't know what to do?" Then ask Him to show you, but don't just sit there and die — wasting away in frustration.

4. We Have to Endure Transition

During times of transition, God is uniquely shaping and equipping us for the next phase of life or ministry. There is a period during childbirth that is called transition. It comes right before the actual birth and is characterized by intense contractions and almost complete cervical dilation. At transition, there is no going back.

Ironically, transition is usually the shortest part of labor, lasting 15 minutes to half an hour on average. However, it is also the most intense part for many women. Likewise, spiritually it is often just before we break forth into a new level that is the most intense. Notice it is right after his baptism and just before He launches his public ministry and calls His disciples that Jesus is called to a 40-day fast and tempted by the enemy in the wilderness. In childbirth, the major emotional sign for the transition stage is feeling like giving up. Many of us give up during transition instead of crying out to God for the strength to bring forth what He is doing in our lives. Transition is the point where we feel the most like giving up, but we are the closest to complete deliverance.

Isaiah 66:9-14 KJV

9 Shall I bring to the birth, and not cause to bring forth? saith the LORD: shall I cause to bring forth, and shut the womb? saith thy God. 10 Rejoice ye with Jerusalem, and be glad with her, all ye that love her: rejoice for joy with her, all ye that mourn for her: 11 That ye may suck, and be satisfied with the breasts of her consolations; that ye may milk out, and be delighted with the abundance of her glory. 12 For thus saith the LORD, Behold, I will extend peace to her like a river, and the glory of the Gentiles like a flowing stream: then shall ye suck, ye shall be borne upon her sides, and be dandled upon her knees. 13 As one whom his mother comforteth, so will I comfort you; and ye shall be comforted in Jerusalem. 14 And when ye see this, your heart shall rejoice, and your bones shall flourish like an herb: and the hand of the LORD shall be known toward his servants, and his indignation toward his enemies.

Isaiah 66:9-14 NIV

9 Do I bring to the moment of birth and not give delivery?" says the Lord. "Do I close up the womb when I bring to delivery?" says your God. *10* "Rejoice with Jerusalem and be glad for her, all you who love her; rejoice greatly with her, all you who mourn over her. *11* For you will nurse and be satisfied at her comforting breasts; you will drink deeply and delight in her overflowing abundance." *12* For this is what the Lord says: "I will extend peace to her like a river, and the wealth of nations like a flooding stream; you will nurse and be carried on her arm and dandled on her knees. *13* As a mother comforts her child, so will I comfort you; and you will be comforted over Jerusalem." *14* When you see this, your heart will rejoice and you will flourish like grass; the hand of the Lord will be made known to his servants, but his fury will be shown to his foes.

Each of us must decide if we are going to be who God says we are and accomplish what God created us to do or are we going to be who people and circumstances try to determine we are. This is the time, the strategic time, the kairos time, to move into your new territory, your new level of authority, your new manifestations of the will and promises of God in your life. God gives us the strength to take one step forward, the potential to climb one more rung in the ladder.

In the vision, the Lord was revealing that He desires for us to become more and more like Him. That transition or transformation process is not an easy one. At times, it is painful and frustrating. It may even frequently seem impossible, but as we abide in Him and allow His Word to abide in us, we are gradually being transformed. Like in the vision, we have to stand in the flame that is His Presence and allow Him to strip away everything that is not like Him. We have to allow Him to polish our hearts, re-make our character, and shave away our other dependencies. If we endure the transformation or transition process, we can become vessels that carry His Glory and reflect His Presence to all who look upon us.

At Your Feet

At Your feet I can cast all my cares
On Your shoulders I can rest every burden
On Your chest I can lay my head and find peace
On Your garments can fall my every tear of sorrow
On Your faithfulness I can depend
In Your love I can abide
In Your grace I can find comfort
In Your presence I can receive joy
Unto You I can commit my life

Conclusion—The Heart of the Matter

King David went in, took his place before God, and prayed: "Who am I, my Master God, and what is my family, that you have brought me to this place in life? But that's nothing compared to what's coming, for you've also spoken of my family far into the future, given me a glimpse into tomorrow, my Master God! What can I possibly say in the face of all this? You know me, Master God, just as I am. You've done all this not because of who I am but because of who you are — out of your very heart! — but you've let me in on it. —2 Samuel 7:18 MSG

But even there, if you seek God, your God, you'll be able to find him if you're serious, looking for him with your whole heart and soul. —Deut. 4:29a MSG

Just make sure you stay alert. Keep close watch over your-
selves. Don't forget anything of what you've seen. Don't
let your heart wander off. Stay vigilant as long as you live.
Teach what you've seen and heard to your children and-
grandchildren. —Deut. 4:9 MSG

We have to receive a revelation of who God is and what it means to be a son or daughter of God. It is in our understanding the heart of our Spiritual Father towards us that we can truly begin to understand ourselves and our God-given rights and privileges. We need to know that we are beloved. We are His Jedidiah. We need to know that we are the apple of His eye. We need to know that we are special to Him. We are not special to Him because of what we have. We are special to Him because of who we are — His Beloved Children. And we have a right to every promise our Father has made to us. And we have the right to fight and destroy any ungodly spirit that would try to keep it from us. God will withhold no good thing from us.

Acts 13:22
And when he had removed him, he raised up unto them David to be their king; to whom also he gave testimony, and said, I have found David the son of Jesse, a man after mine own heart, which shall fulfil all my will.

Understanding why David was a man after God's own heart begins with a basic comparison/contrast between Saul, Israel's first king, and David, Israel's second king. The two men served in similar roles but differed drastically in their motivations.

The phrase "after God's own heart" depicts someone dedicated to his/her own will to someone who surrenders his/her will to God's plans. Someone dedicated to his/her own will seek to justify his/her actions. The person dedicated to God's will has already accepted a truth about himself/herself: "Without God, I am nothing. In my life, there is never a question about Who is in charge of my life."

In this contrast, it is evident that Saul and David are significantly different men. David wanted a relationship with God. He was internally motivated. Saul wanted the advantages of association with God. His selfish motives and desire to please people are clearly revealed in his rash and self-serving acts. This reveals a powerful lesson for us. Too many people want to be associated with God for the benefits or blessings. What God seeks are those people who want relationships with Him because they belong to Him. God seeks people who serve Him by surrendering themselves rather than people who seek to connect with Him for selfish reasons.

A person after God's heart is someone who seeks after the heart of God. It is someone who desires to know Him intimately and to love Him passionately.

Psalm 78:70-72

[70]He chose David also his servant, and took him from the sheepfolds:

[71]From following the ewes great with young he brought him to feed Jacob his people, and Israel his inheritance.

[72]So he fed them according to the integrity of his heart; and guided them by the skillfulness of his hands.

It is someone who has integrity of heart. That does not mean a person after God's own heart will never make a mistake. David made many mistakes including both adultery and murder. But it does mean that their heart's desire is to do right. Their heart is to do His Will. Psalm 78:72 says that David fed the people of God according to the integrity of his heart. The Message translation of this verse states:

His good heart made him a good shepherd; he guided the people wisely and well.

David's heart towards God made him a good shepherd and allowed him to guide the people with wisdom.

Genesis 1:26-27 says we are made in His image, in the likeness of God. Psalm 139:13-16 says we are fearfully and wonderfully made, and all the days of our lives were written in God's book before we were ever born, confirming God's prior knowledge and plan for our lives. Ephesians 1:4 states God chose His children before the foundations of the earth were ever formed. In Ephesians 1:13-14, we're told we are God's own possession, chosen for the praise of His glory, and that we have an inheritance in heaven with Him as His children.

But notice the wording in each of the above phrases: "are made," "are fearfully and wonderfully made," "were written," "God chose His children," "we are God's own possession," and "we have an inheritance." These phrases all have one thing in common: they are things done to us or for us by God. These are not things we have done for ourselves; we have not earned or deserved them. We are simply the recipients of "all spiritual blessings in heavenly places in Christ" (Ephesians 1:3). Our worth is given to us by God. We are of immeasurable value to Him because of the price He paid to make us worthy — the death of His Son on the cross.

The Bible tells us that "while we were yet sinners, Christ died for us" (Romans 5:8). In fact, we "were dead in trespasses and sins" (Ephesians 2:1). God imputed to us His own righteousness (2 Corinthians 5:21) not because we were worthy, but because we were unworthy, unlovable, and unable to make ourselves worthy in any way. He actually loved us in spite of our condition (John 3:16), and because He did, we now have infinite worth.

John 1:12 tells us that to those who received Christ and believed in His name, God gave the right to become His children. First John 1:9 tells us that if we confess our sins, He is faithful to forgive our sins and cleanse us from all unrighteousness. If we focus on how much God loves us and the price He paid to redeem us, we'll come to see ourselves as God sees us, and that will help us understand just how much we are really worth as children of the most high God.

Our self-worth is too often based on what other people tell us about ourselves. The one, true authority on our self-worth is Jesus Christ, and since He gave His own life up for us by dying on a cross, that should tell us just how valuable we really are.

Our True Mirror

We often look at ourselves through the mirror of someone else's eyes or through the eyes of our mistakes or our shortcomings. Our true mirror is the Word of God which reflects the image that God has of us and allows us to look at ourselves in the light of His Word, which reveals not only our outer appearance but the state of our hearts. The mirror of God's word reveals our true selves. The mirror of other people's words and our own thoughts will always reveal a distorted image — like a funhouse mirror. It will over-emphasize some things and diminish others to create an image that resembles us but distorts us at the same time. People may hold an opinion of us that is greatly exaggerated. Those who are in the public eye are idealized at times. Some, who have great character, are criticized unjustly. Jesus did not deserve the hateful accusations that were heaped upon him, and Paul suffered a good deal of unmerited character assassination. If they had evaluated themselves through the eyes of others, they would have denied their true selves.

Why did God give me twelve visions of Himself? So that I and all who read this book would come to know Him revealed. We would come into a place of revelation of the Father's heart toward us. As we gain a revelation of who He is, the awesome light of His Presence floods our minds and souls and allows us to finally, truly see who we are in Him. Many of us have viewed God and ourselves through a glass darkly. We are viewing distorted images. We are looking through the eyes of fear, doubt, unbelief, rejection, low self-esteem, or even pride and arrogance. Allow God to take away the distorted images and to reveal to your heart, mind, and very soul — the depth, height, and breadth of His love and heart towards you. And as you rejoice and glory in the light of His Presence, allow Him to show you just how fearfully and wonderfully made you are in His Image and His Likeness.

The Heart of God

This is the heart of God...
To love without fear
To give without agenda
To celebrate without motive
To listen without judgment
To forgive without cause
To be uniquely HIS

My heart...
Has known its share of pain
Has survived its share of wounds
Has endured its share of betrayals
Has been healed and restored by HIS love

CPSIA information can be obtained
at www.ICGtesting.com
Printed in the USA
LVOW03s1945070417

530062LV00001B/3/P